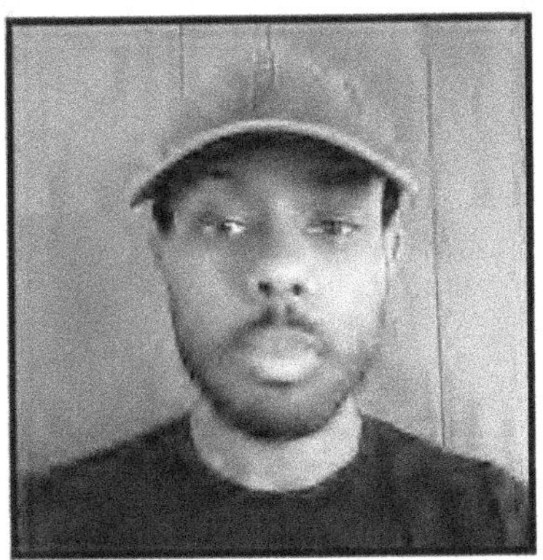

# - About The Author -

I'll like to start this off by saying thank you for your purchase. I'm grateful & humbled by you buying this book. I put alot of time and effort to craft this project.

My name is John C. Spain. I'm from Buffalo, Ny - U.S.A. I've been creating art for many years now. Been in the game for 28 years. Me, my family and teachers first learned of my talents … I want to say … at age 5.

I have a College Degree in the field of Graphic Design from Buffalo State College in 2010. I also attended Erie 1 Boces back in high for graphic design in the early 2000's.

All of my work is created organically. I freestyle and create from the heart. I believe it's the only way to create authentic art.

I made this coloring book for adults, kids, families and friends to use. Have fun, relax, enjoy and use it anyway you want. These books were made for therapeutic
purposes.

johnspainart.com
johnspainart@gmail.com


The best way to find my social media pages is simply going to johnspainart.com and clicking on the social media buttons at the top.  (johnspainart & dynamic.imagination) are my 2 names.

Also I have merchandise for sale by clicking on "Store 1" or "Store 2" on johnspainart.com

DYNAMIC IMAGINATION LLC - 2024

Copyright ©

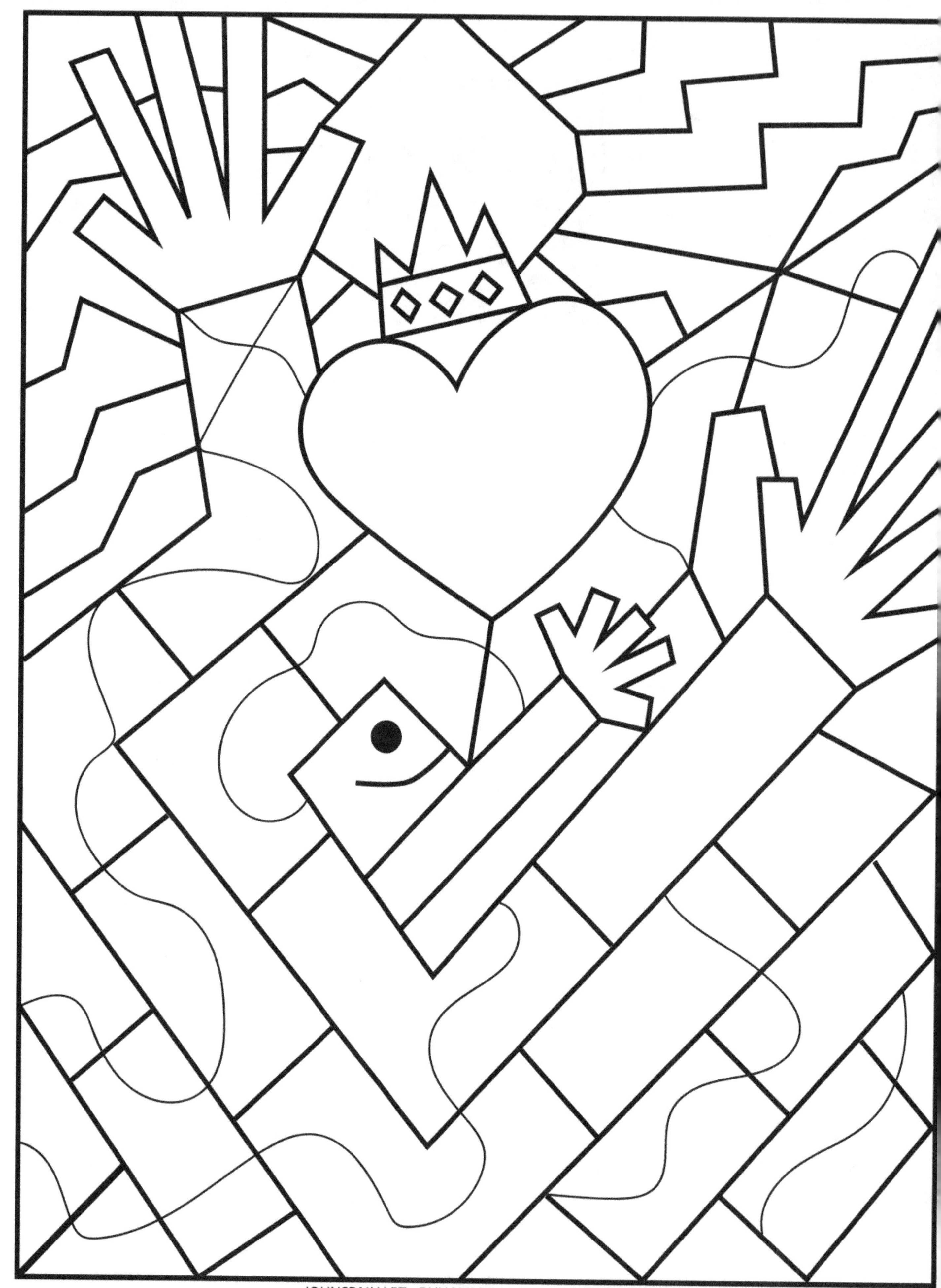

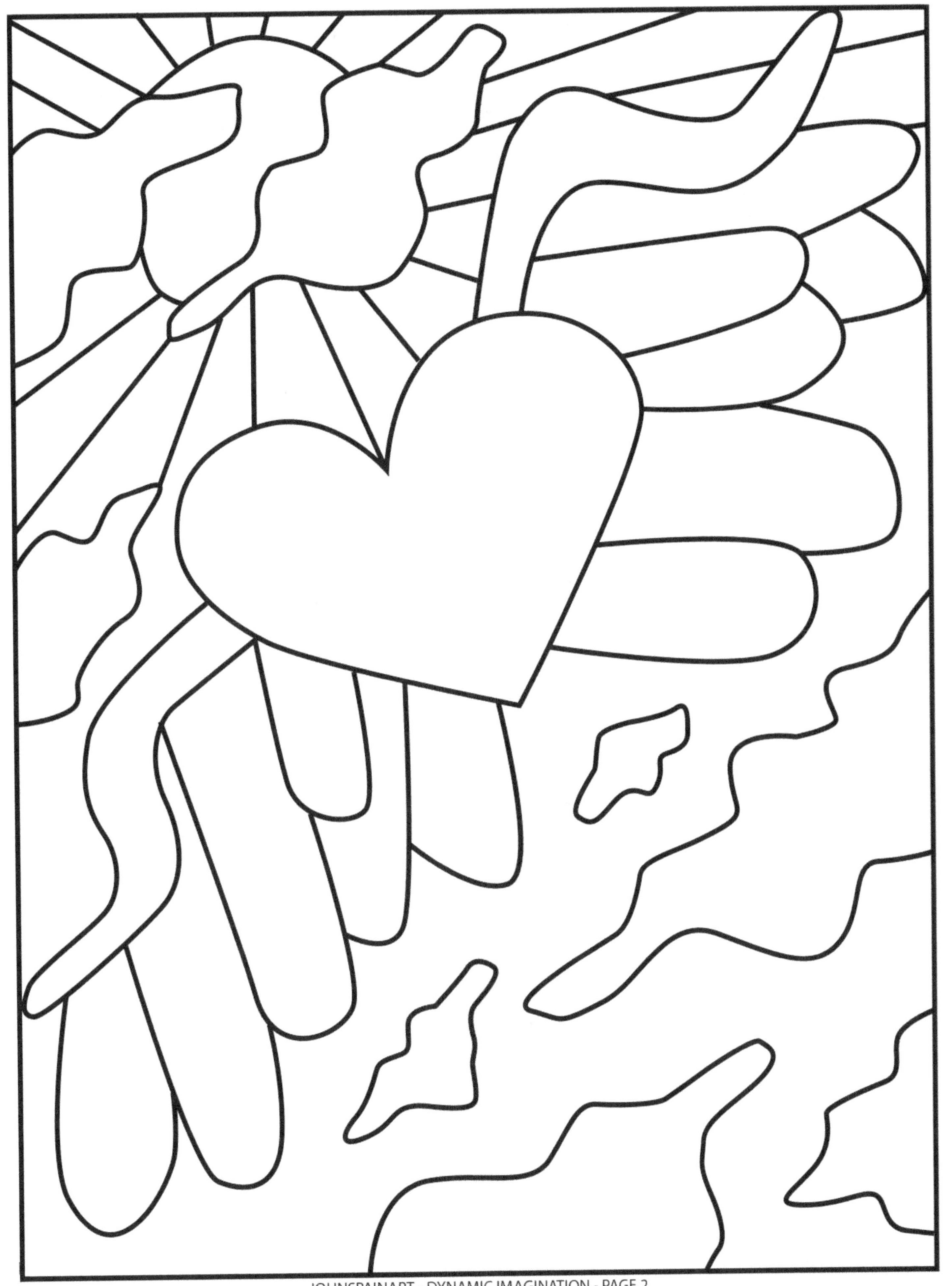

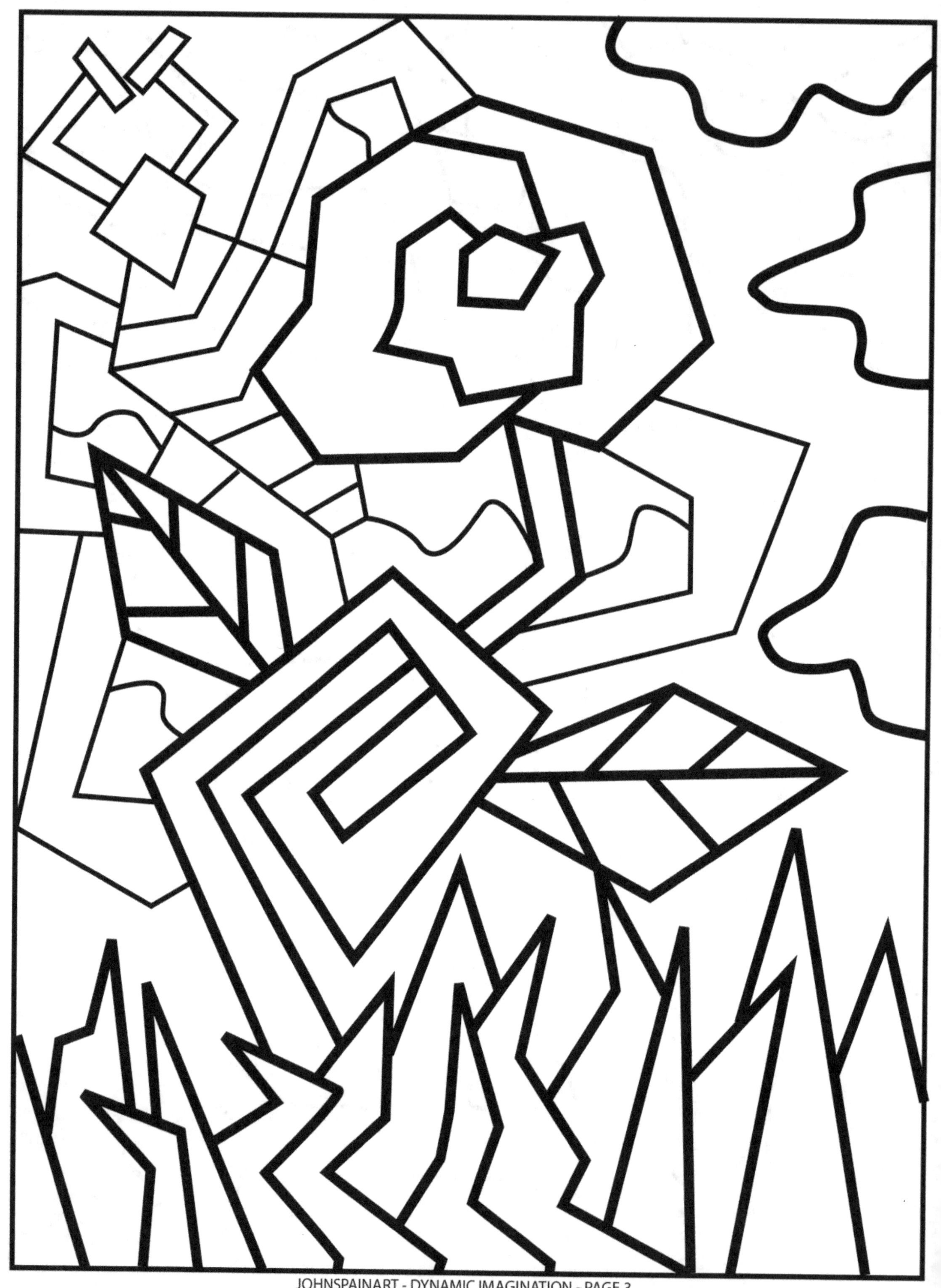

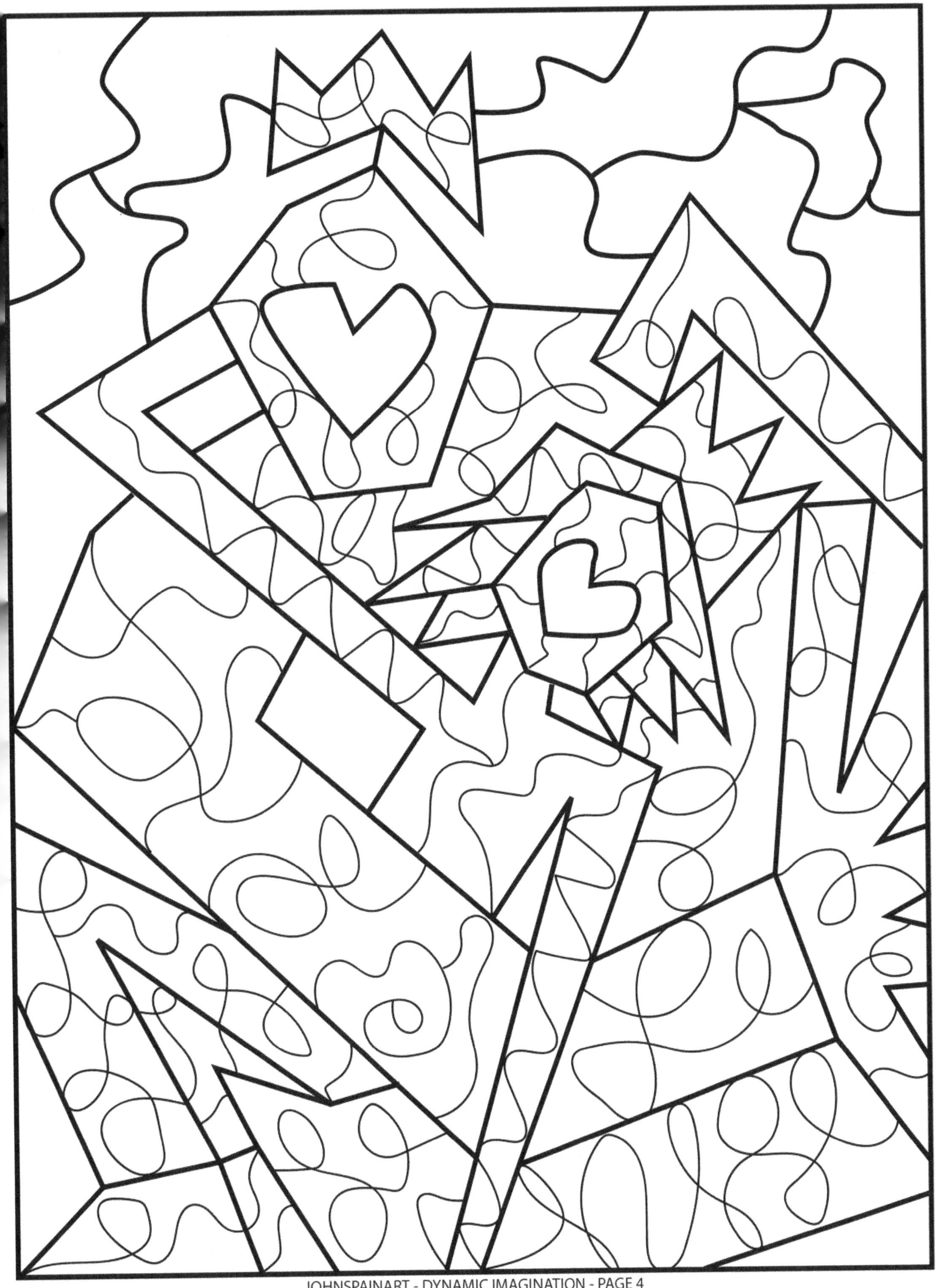

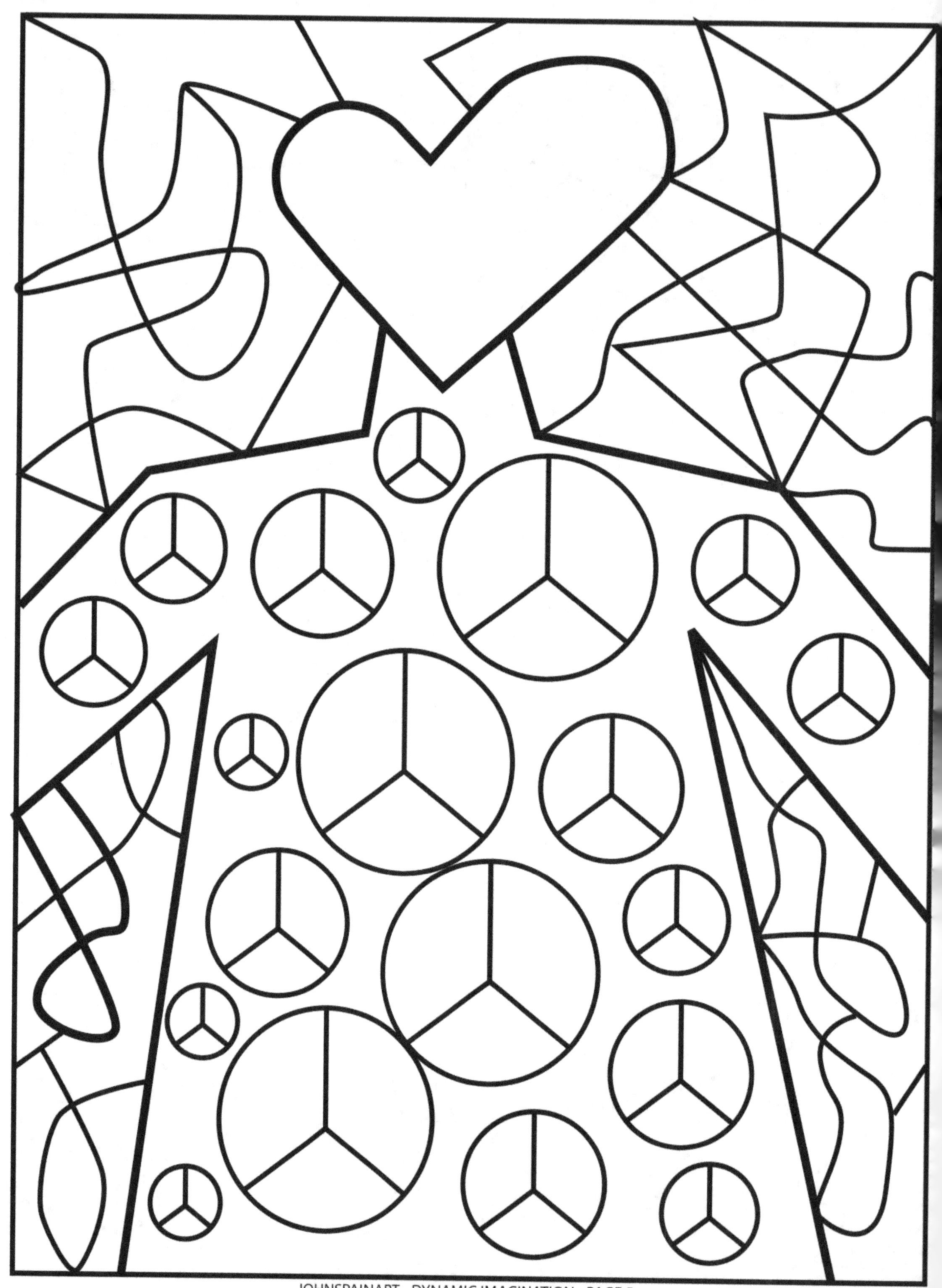

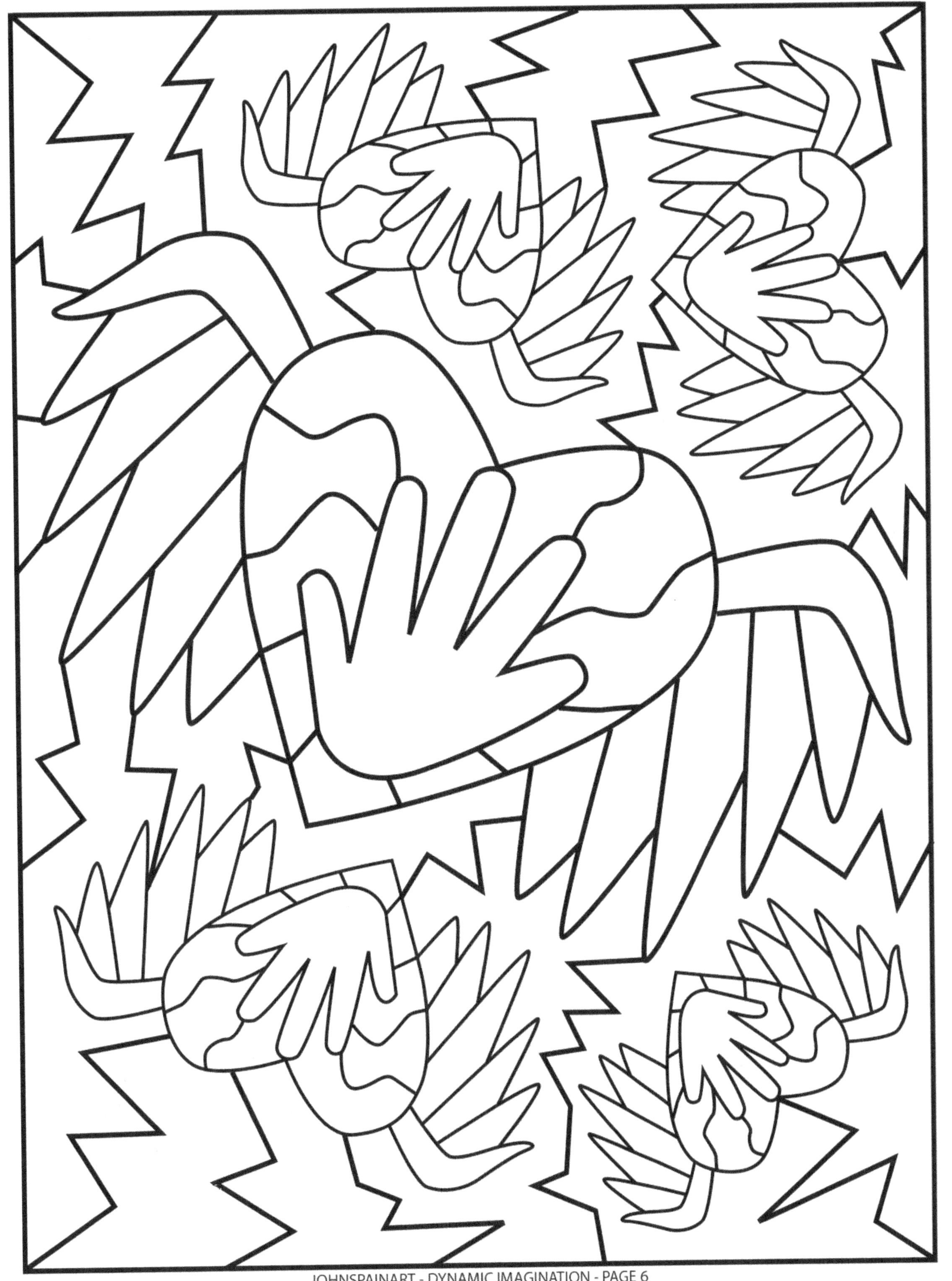

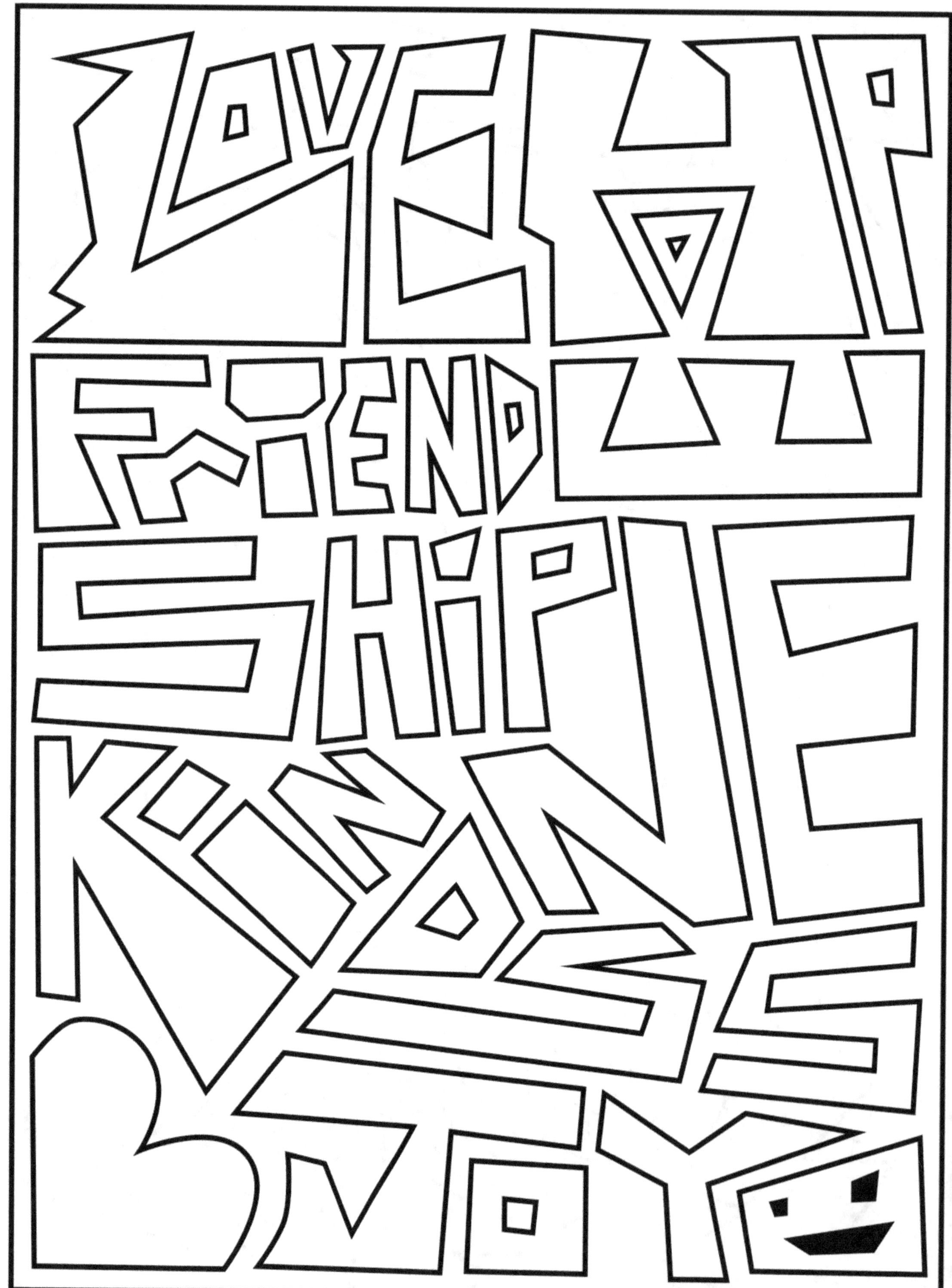

LOVE
FRIENDSHIP
KINDNESS

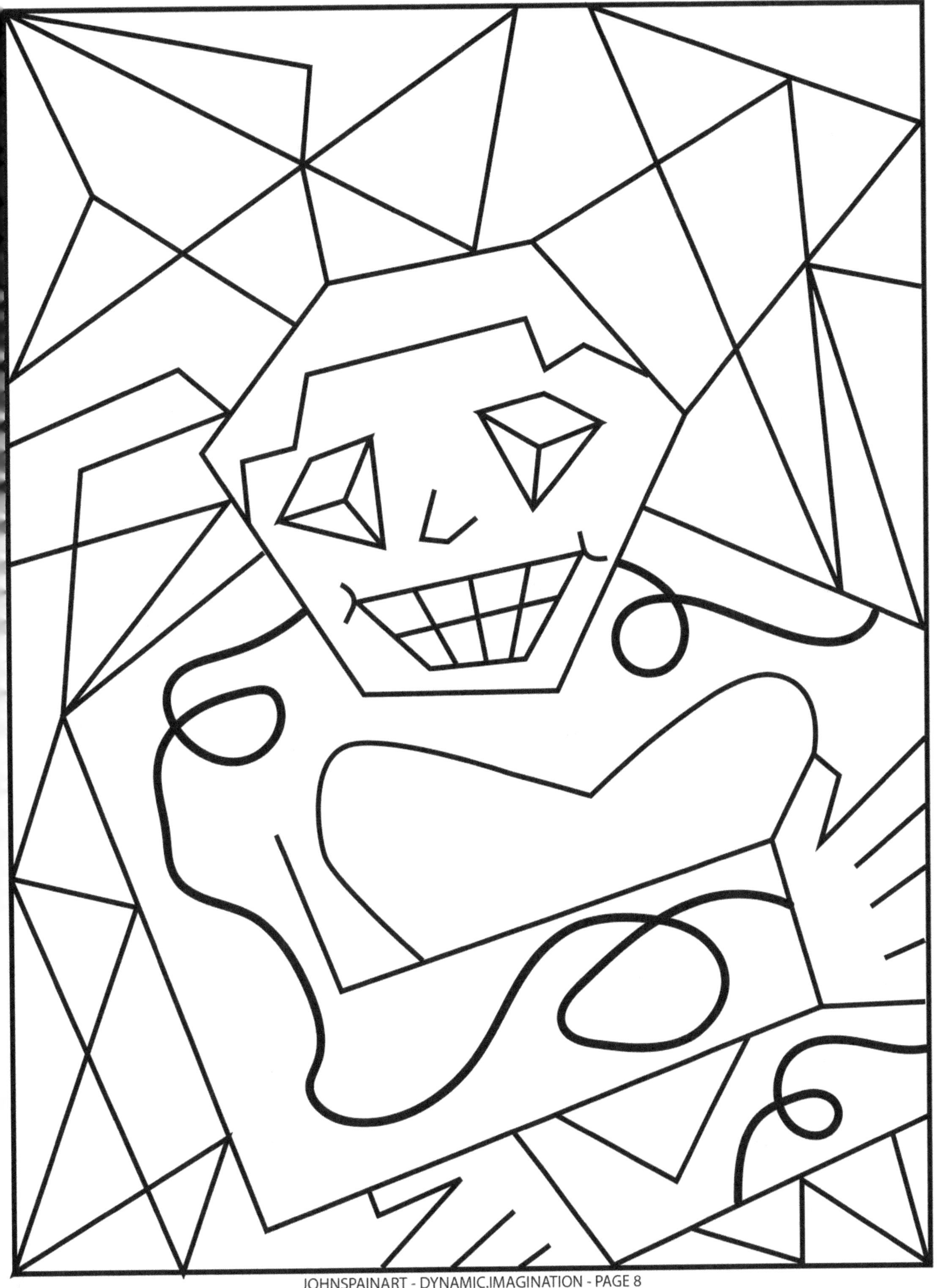

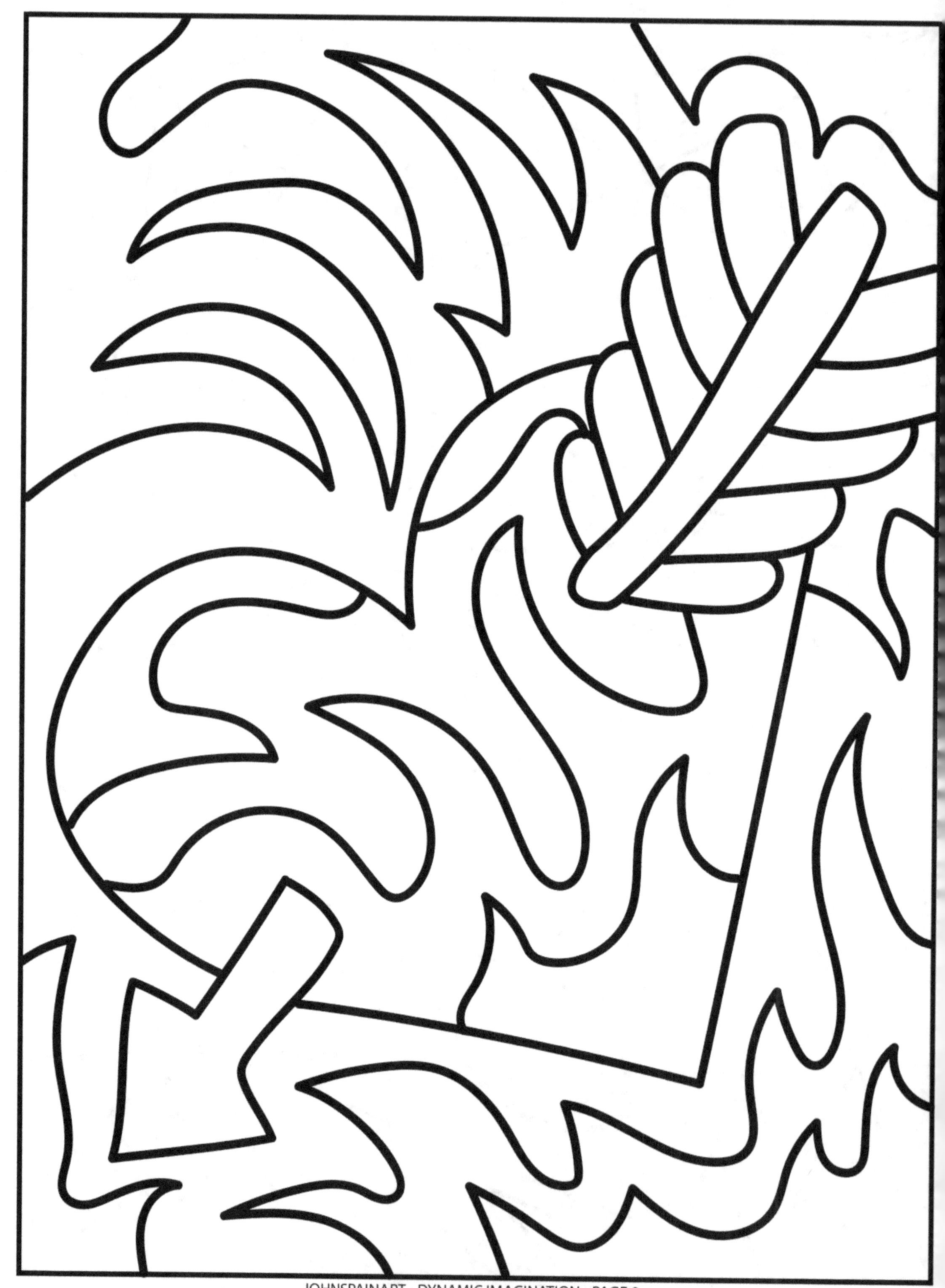

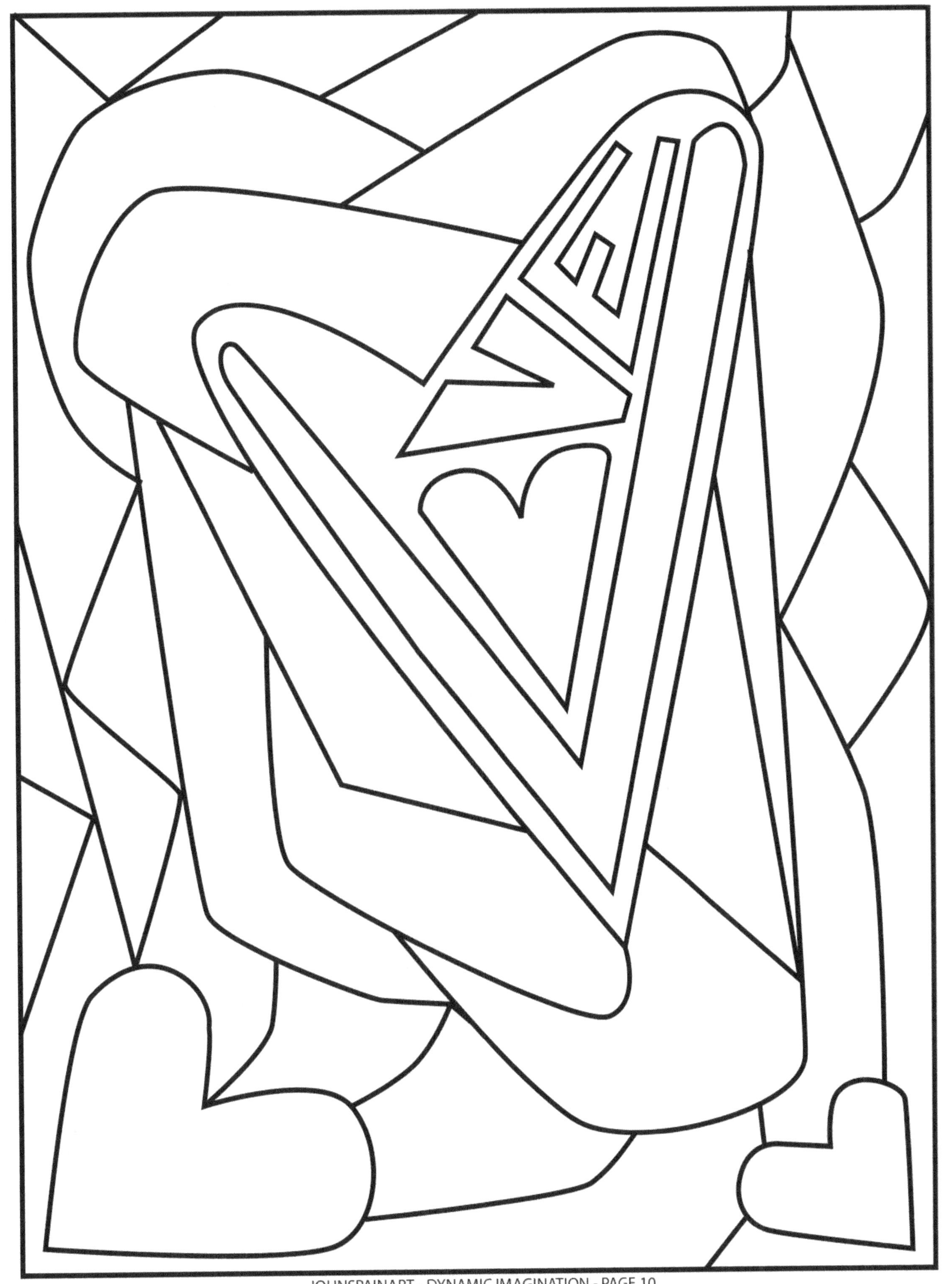

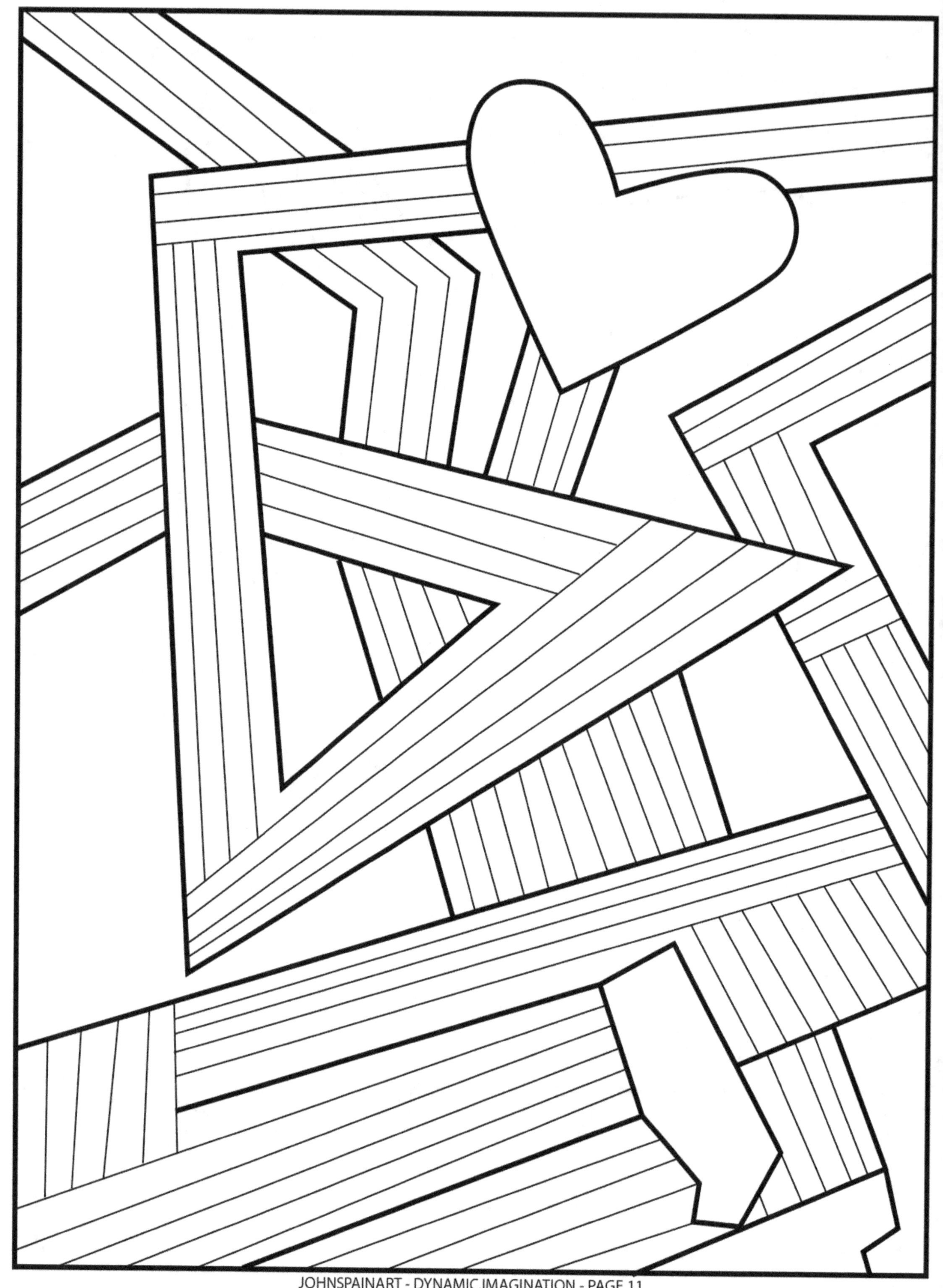

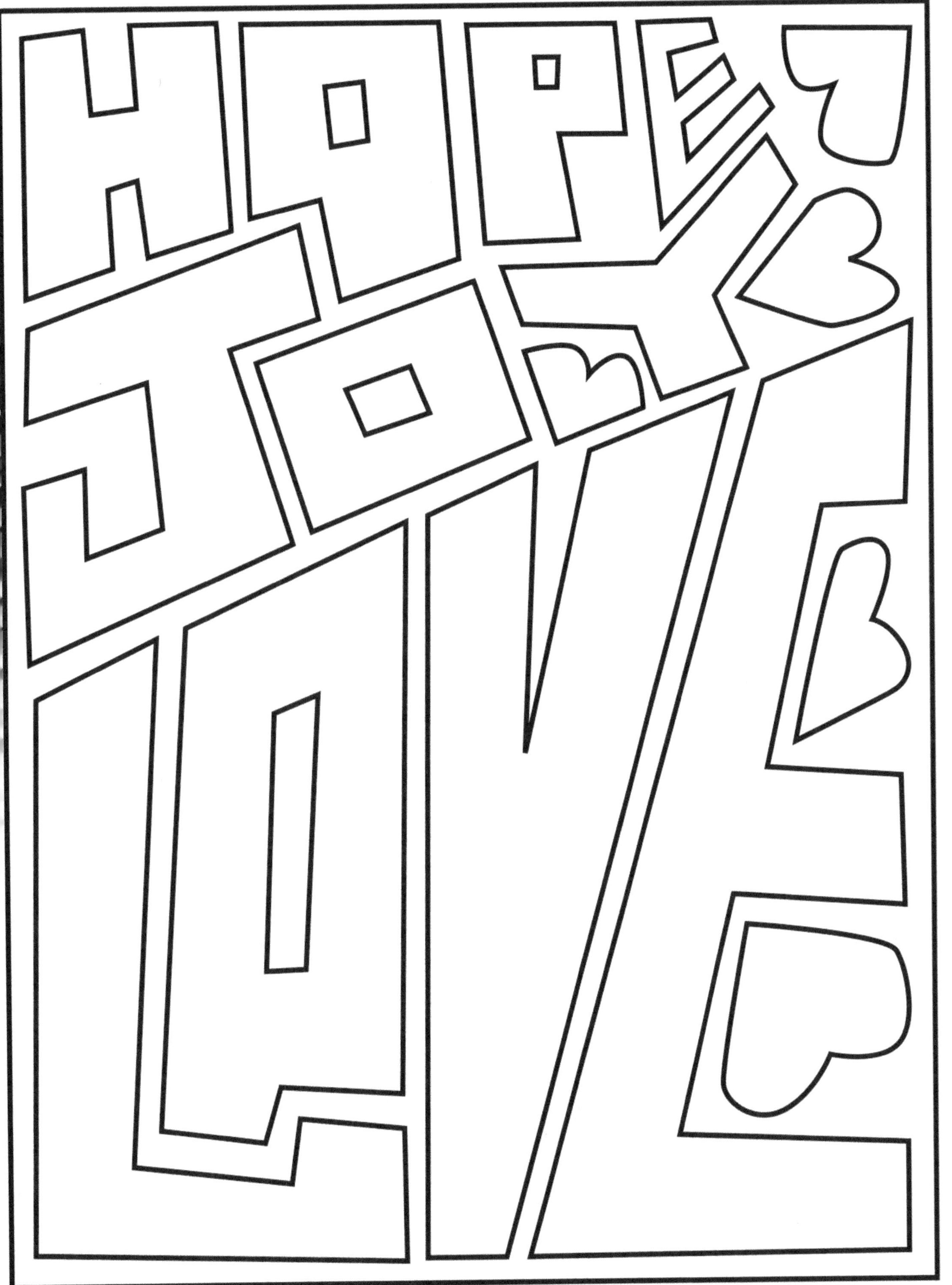

HOPE
JOY
LOVE

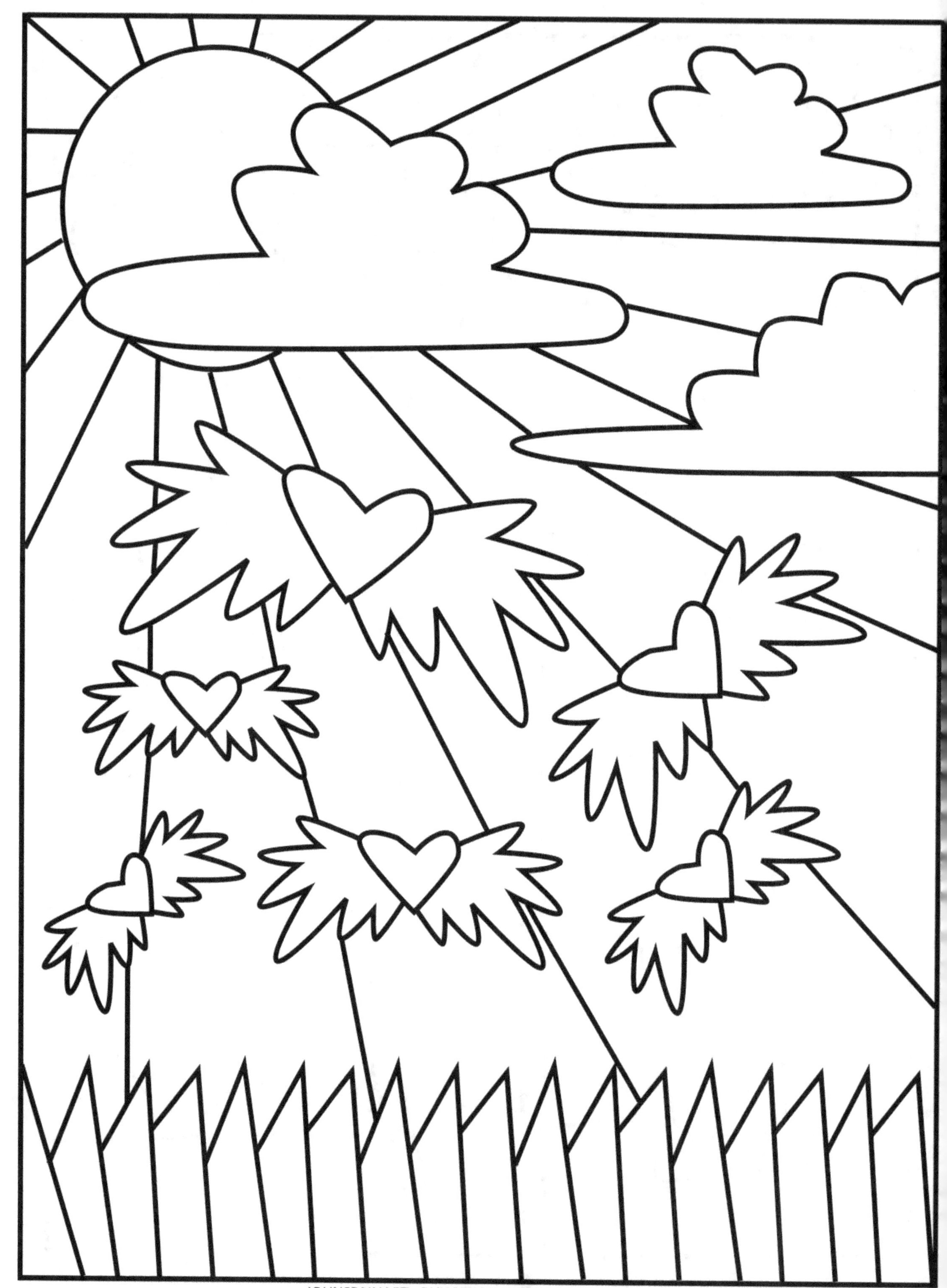

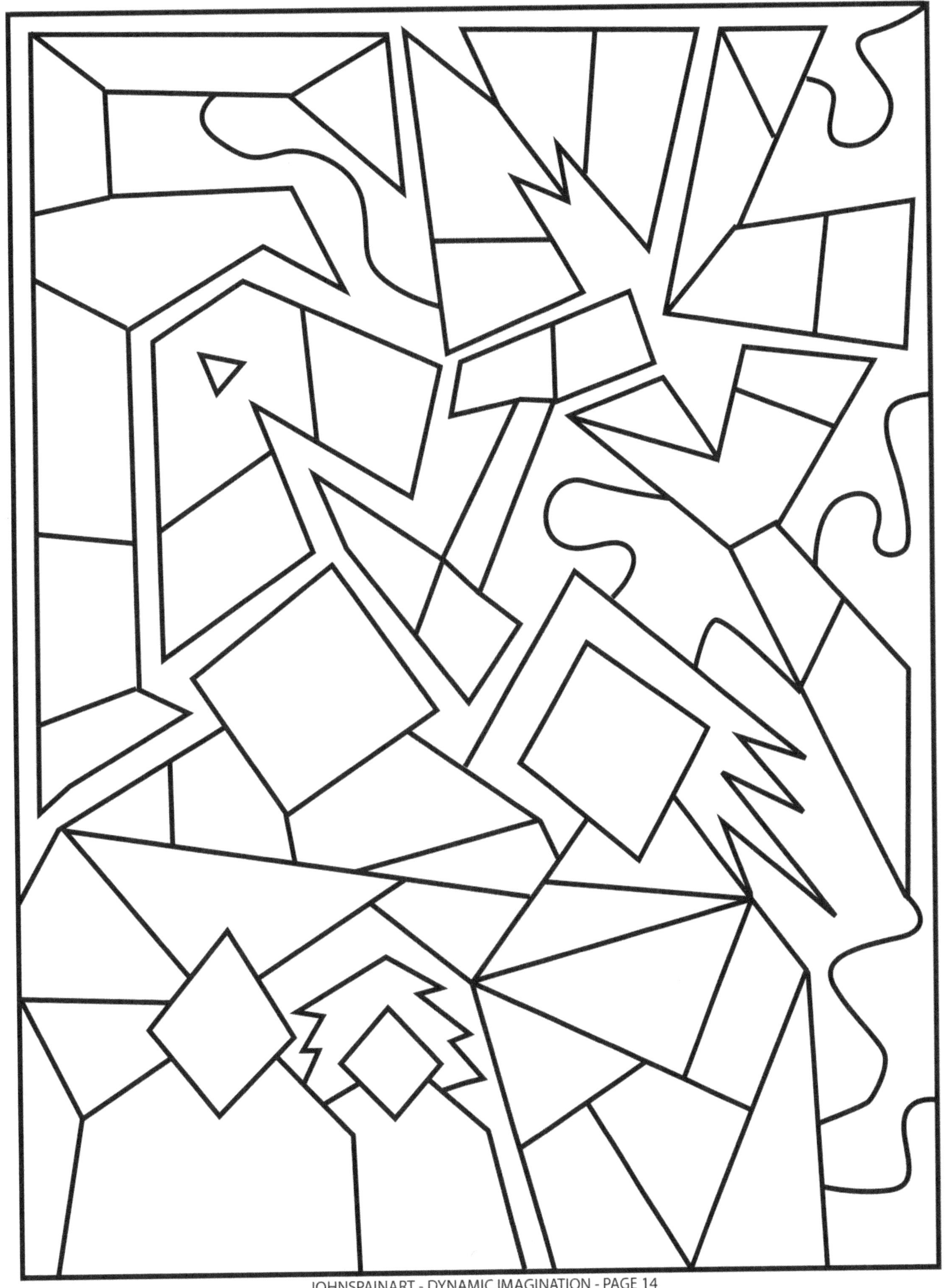

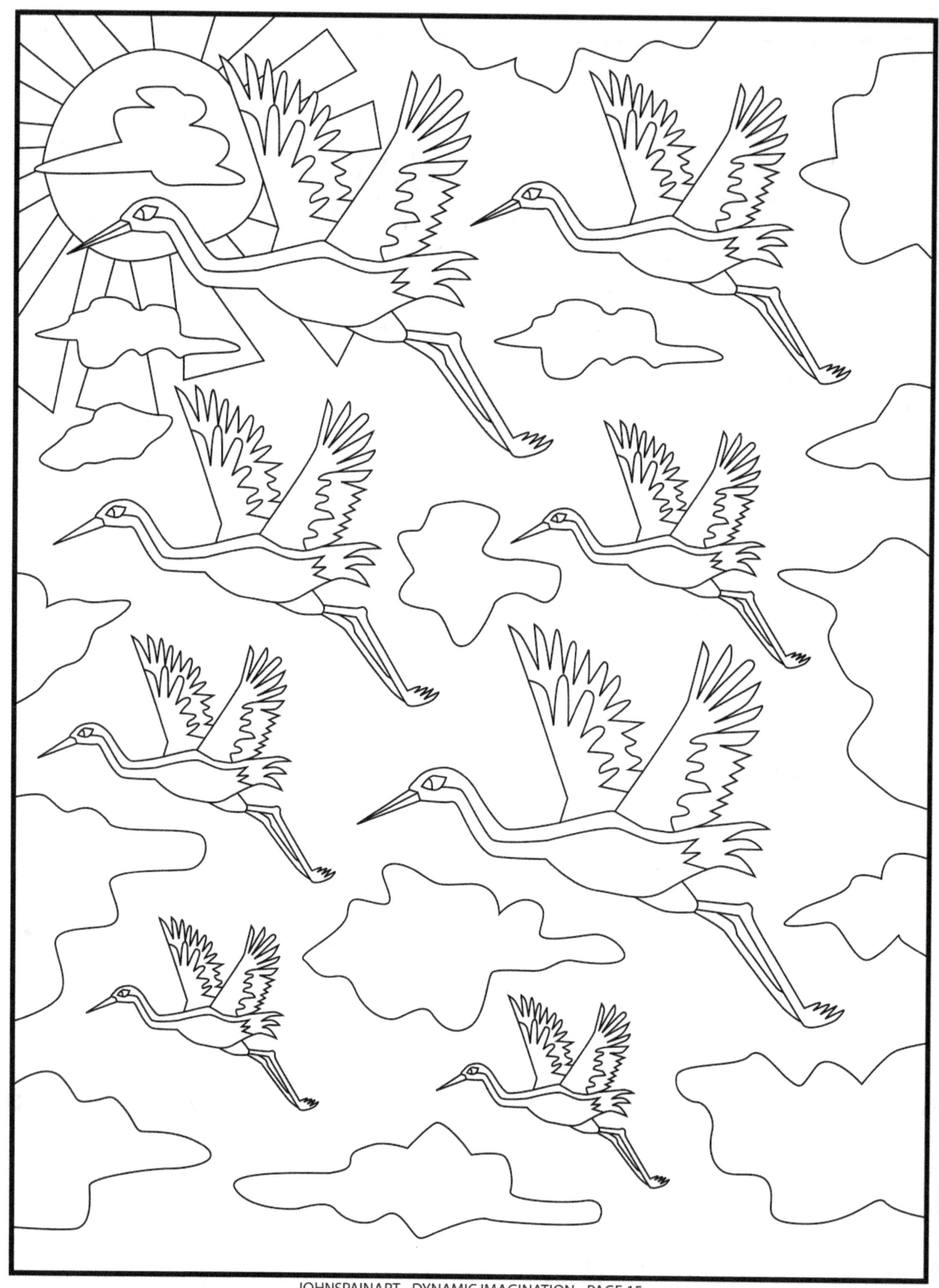

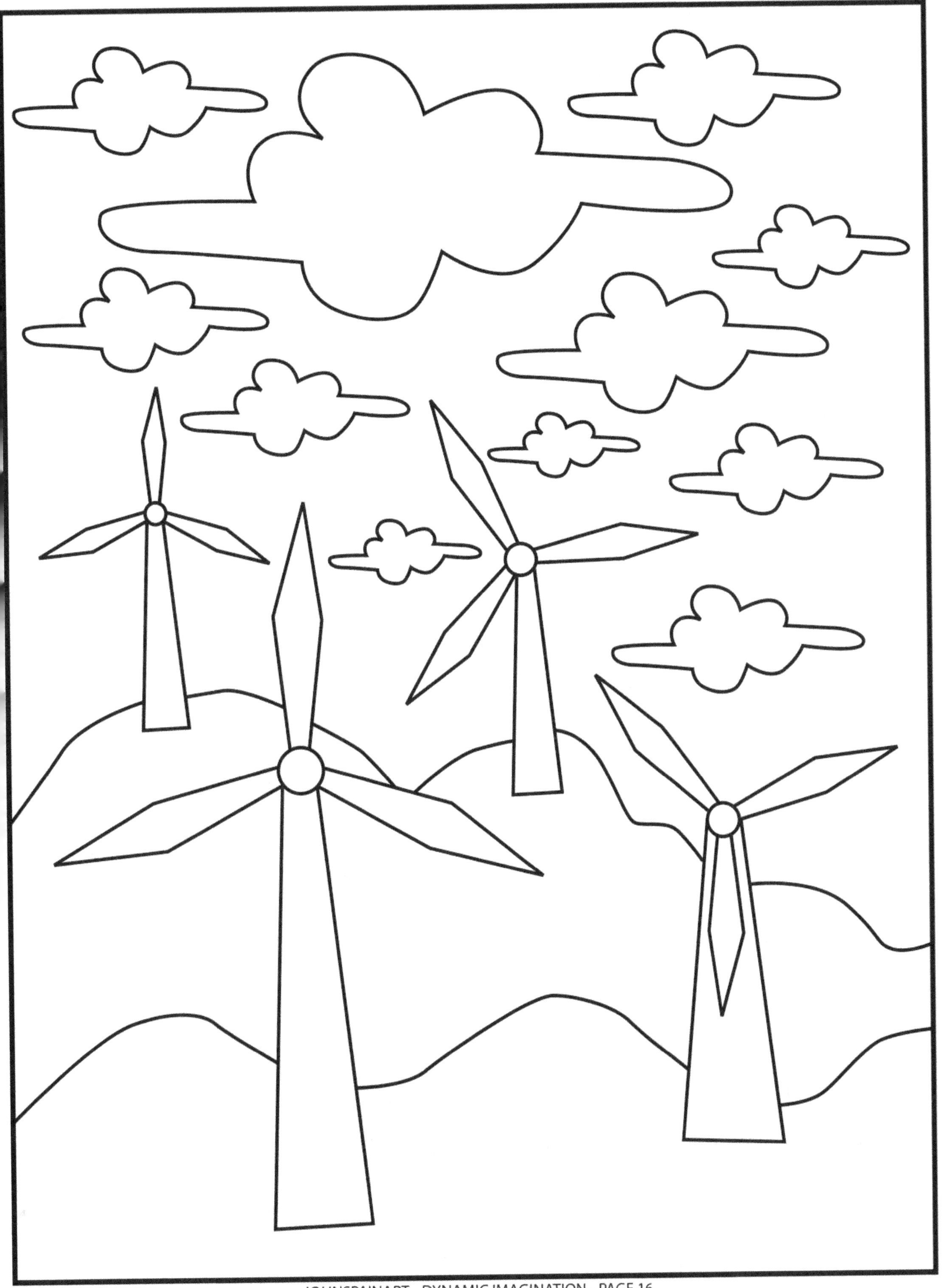

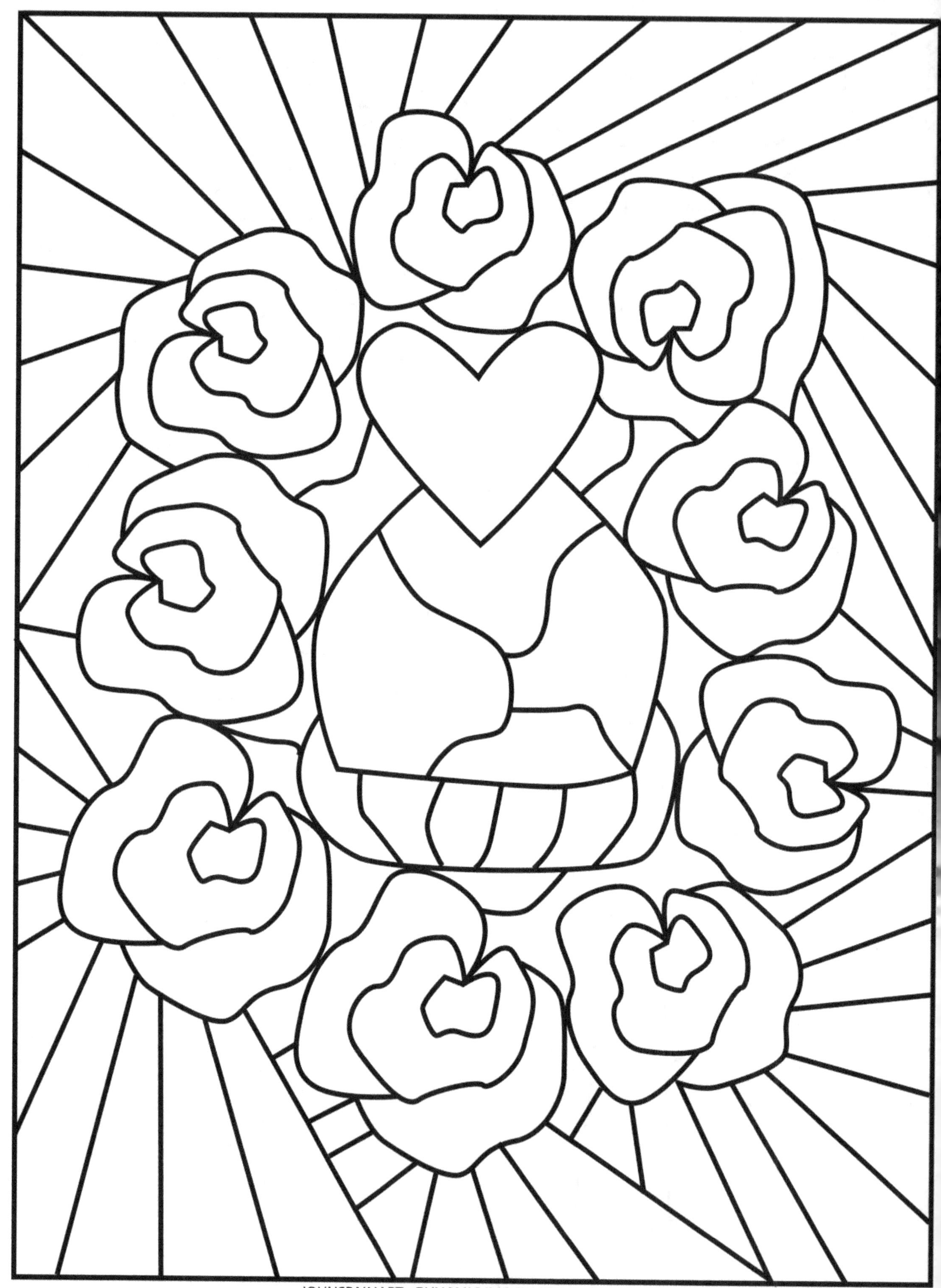

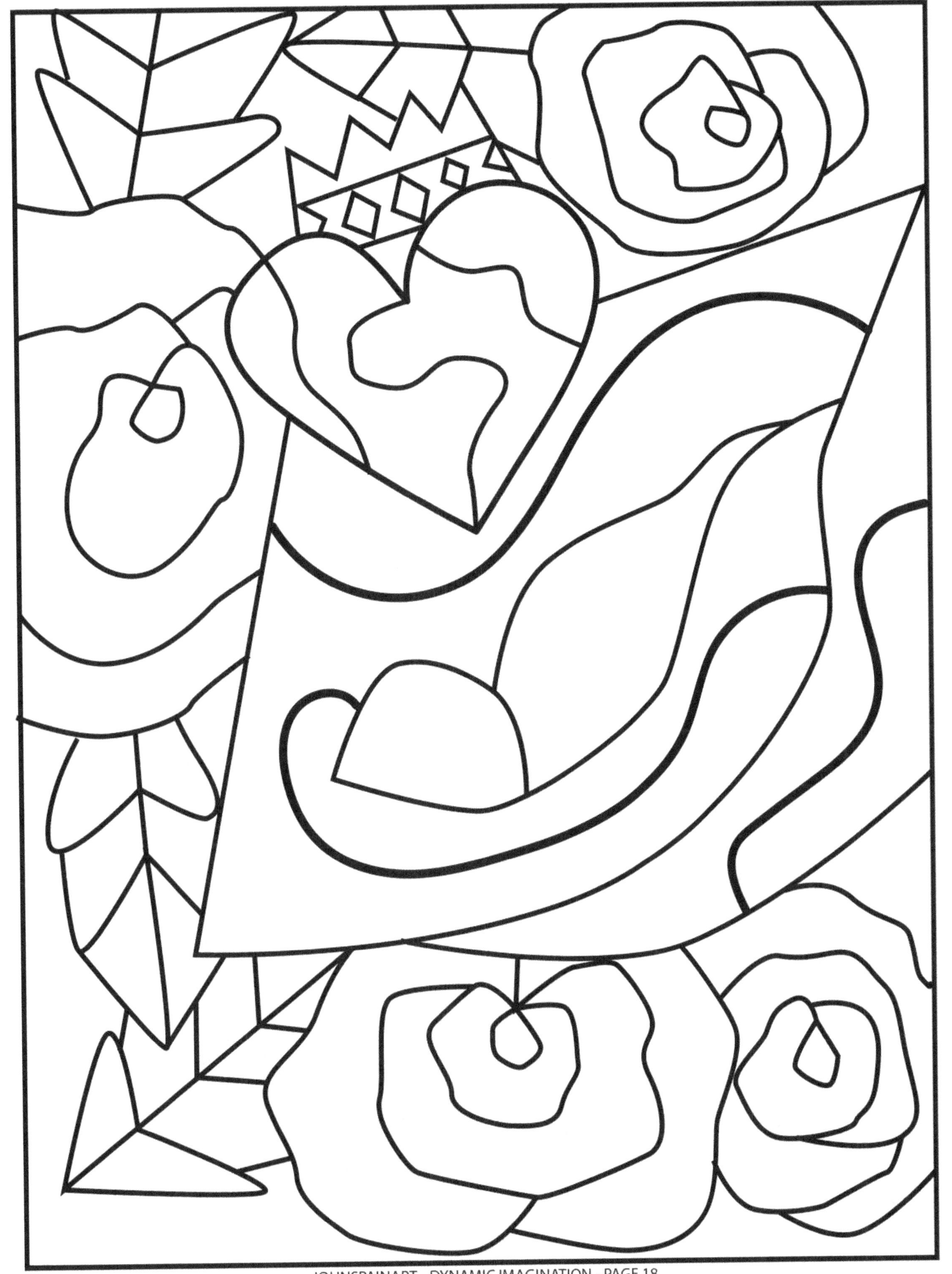

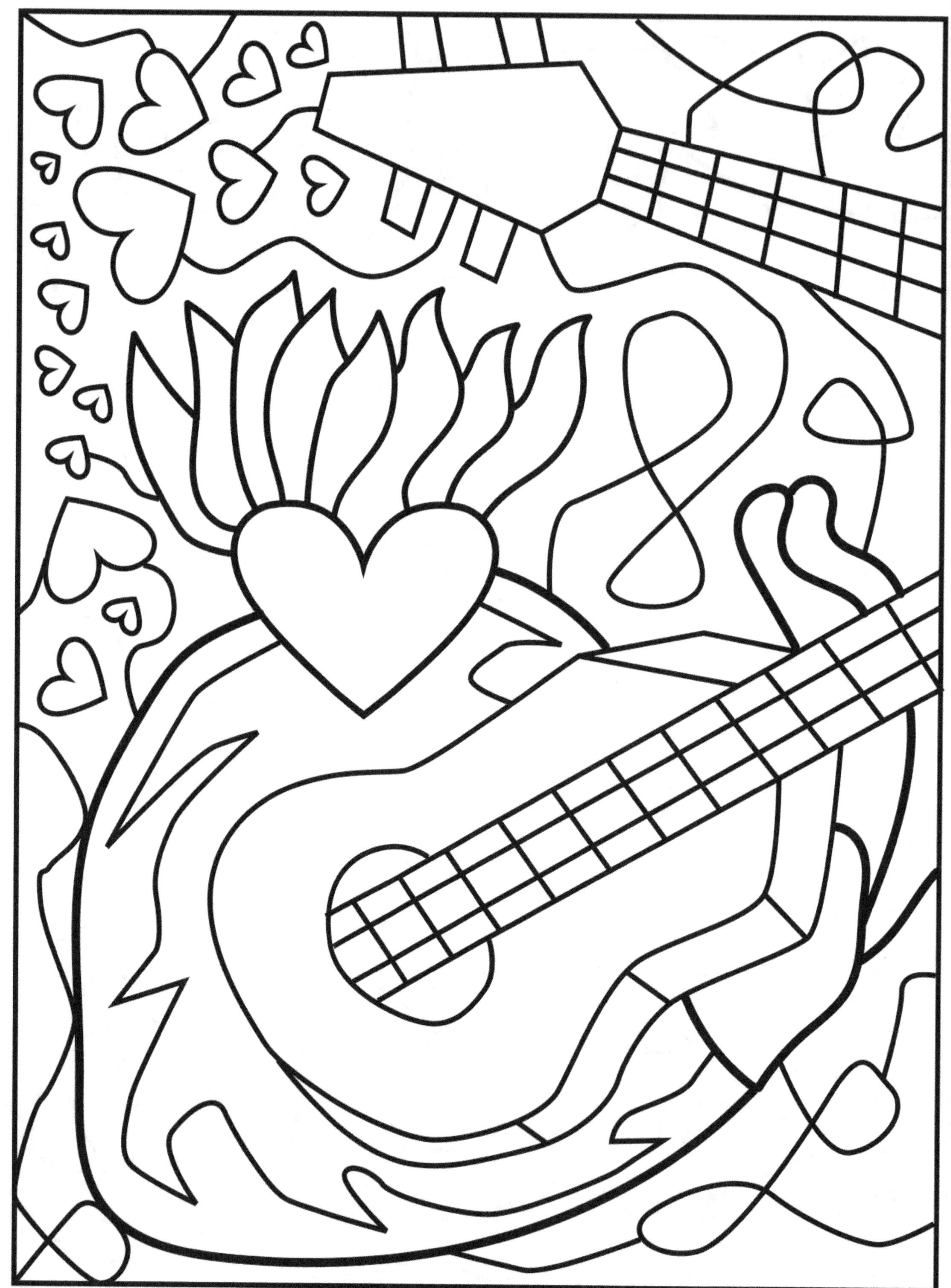

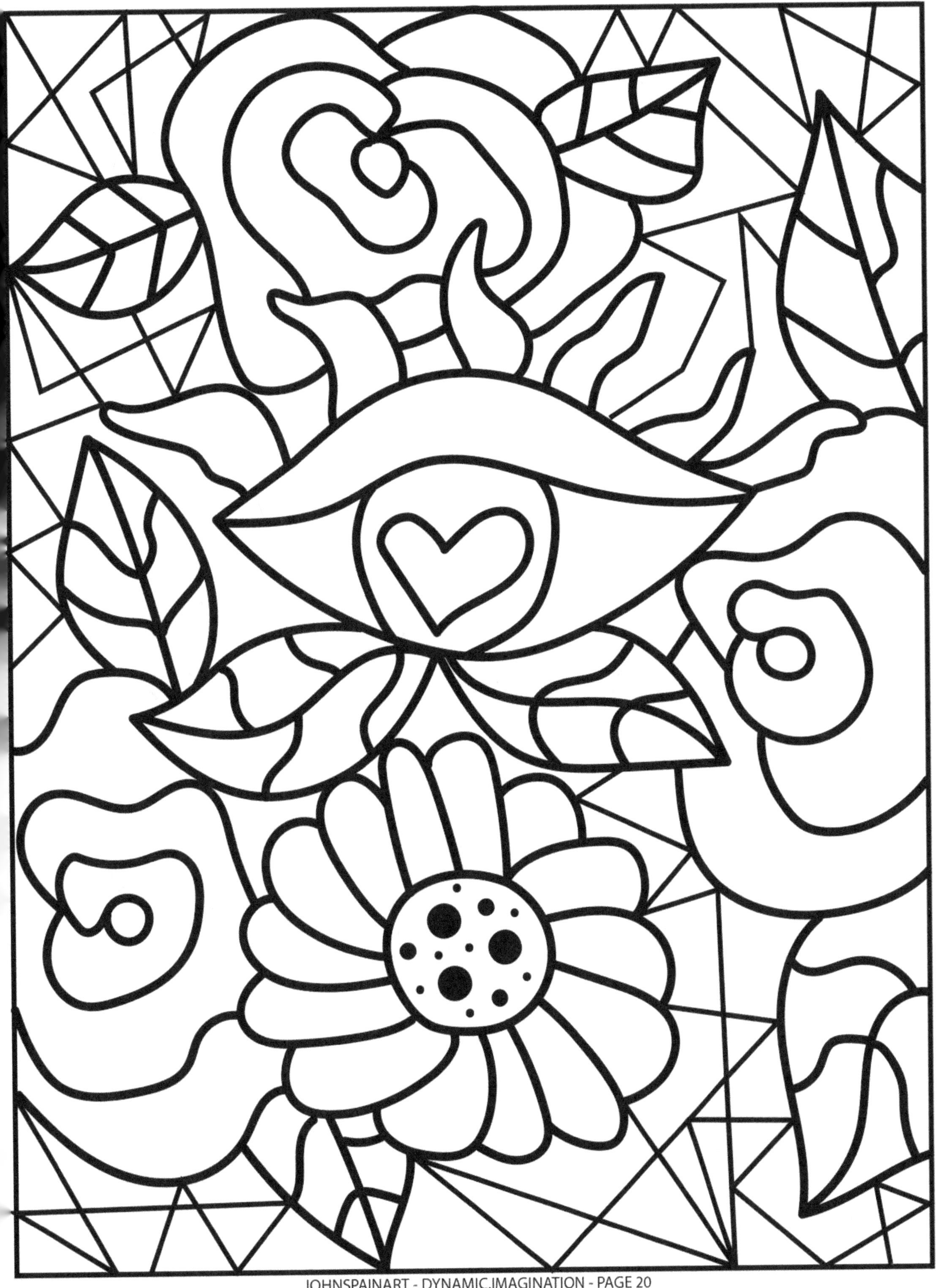

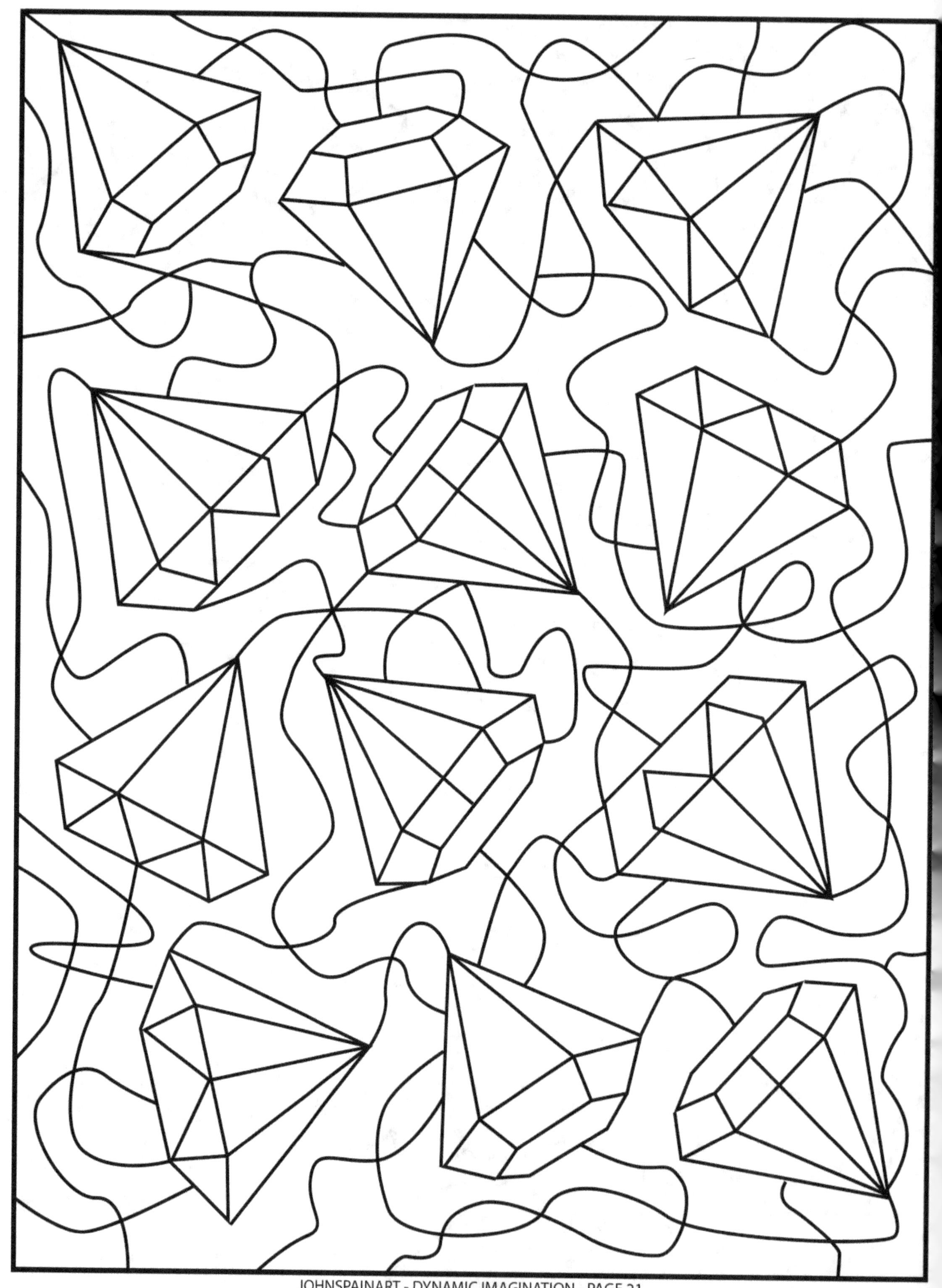

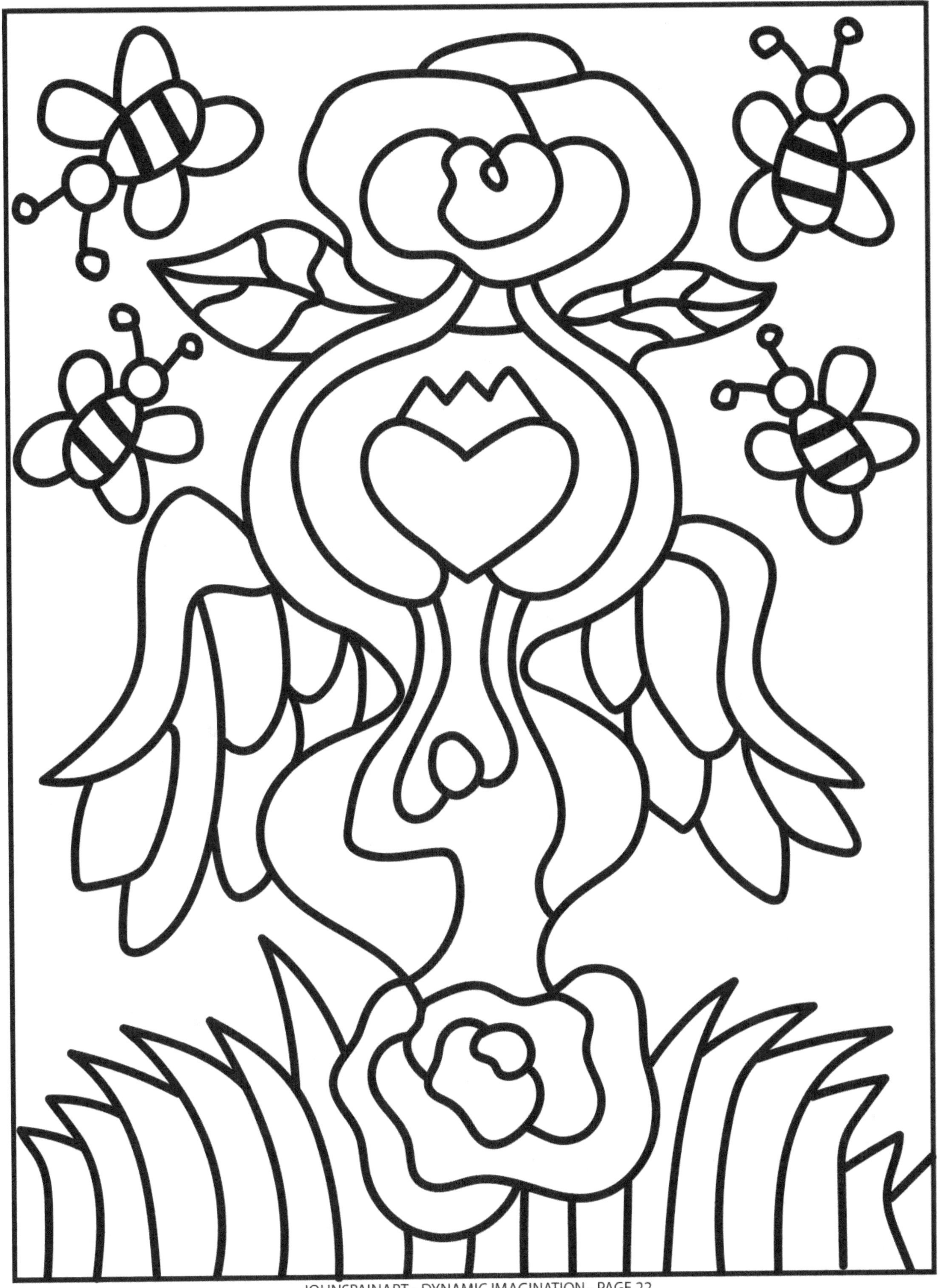

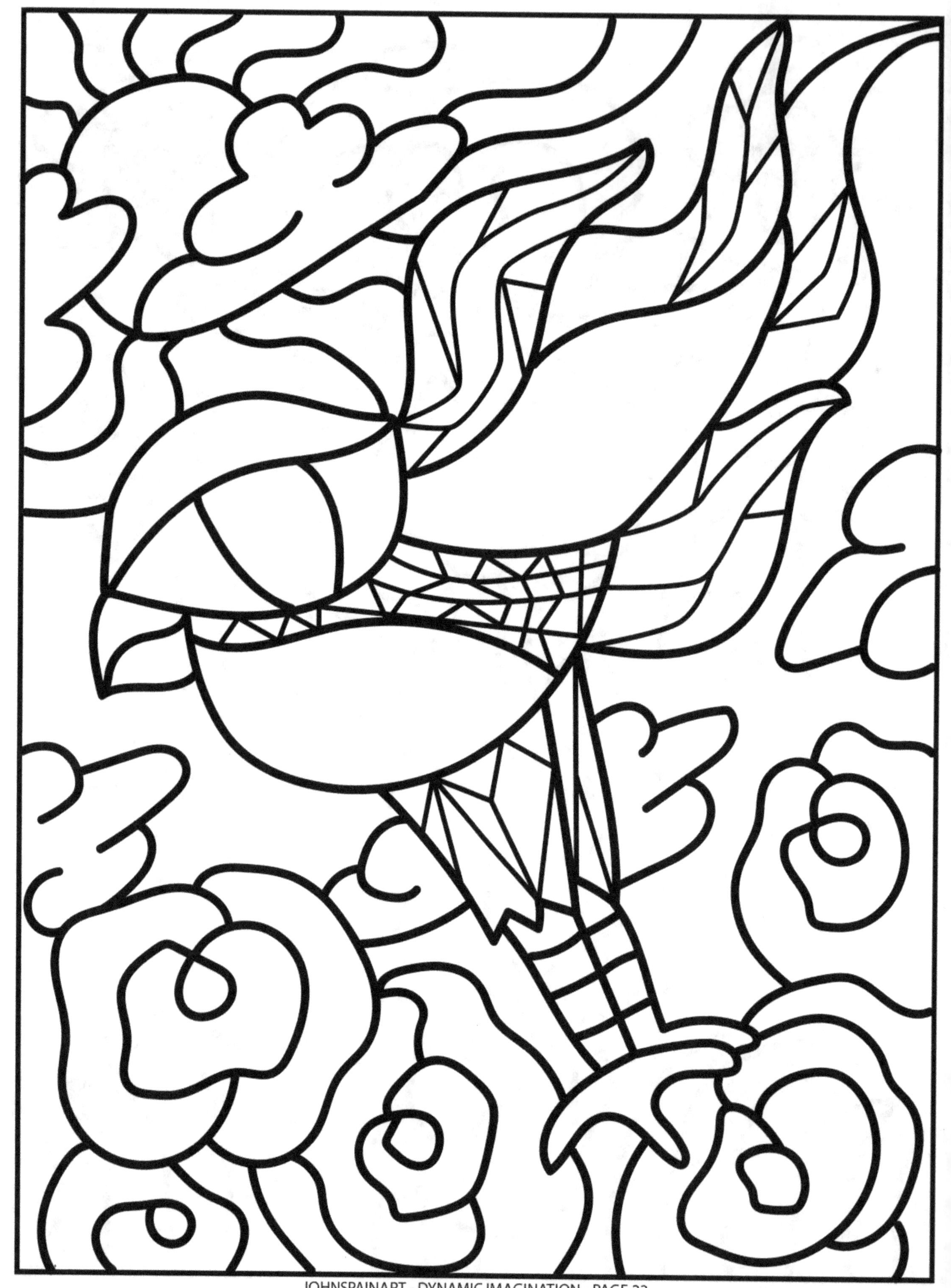

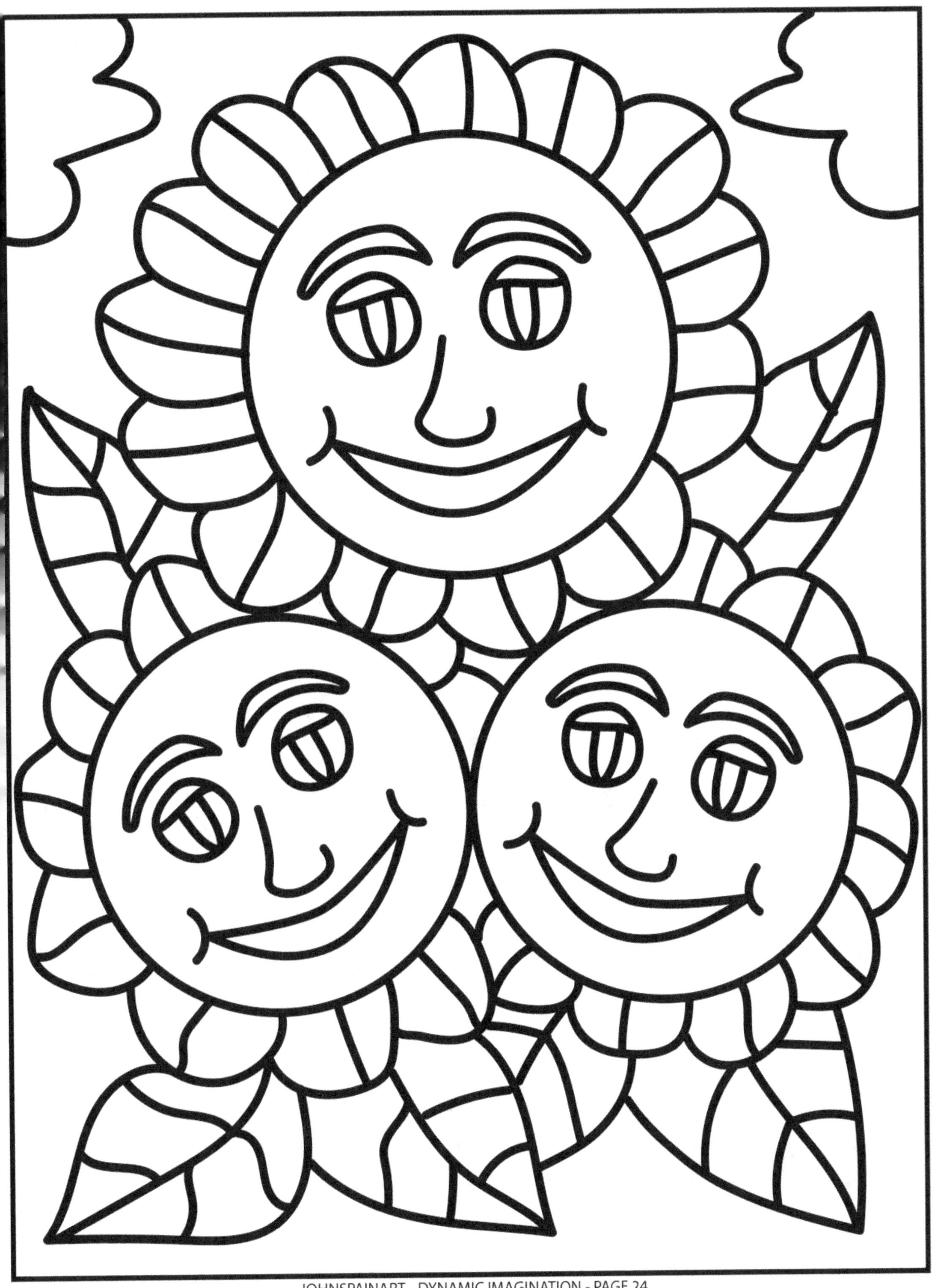

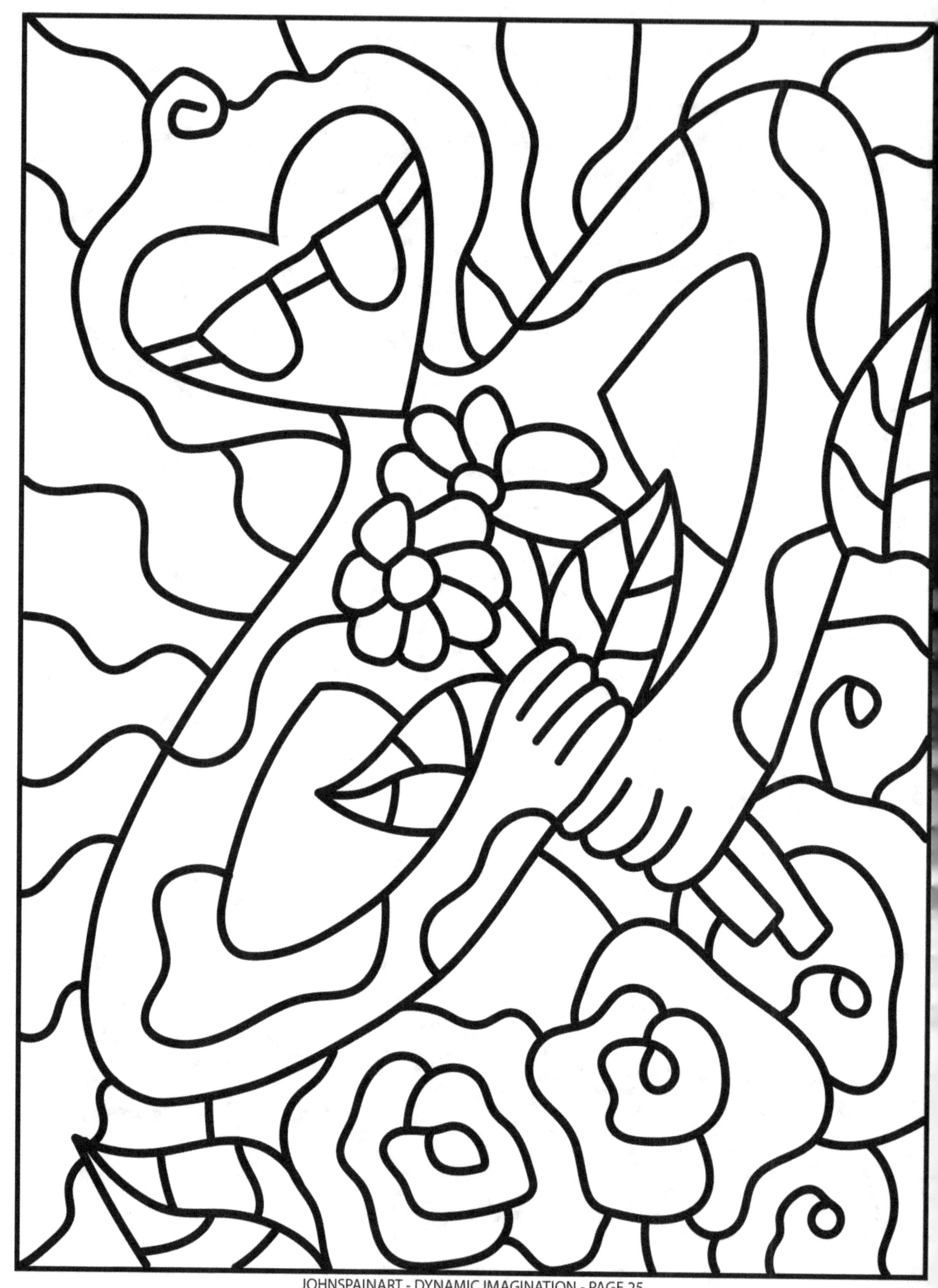

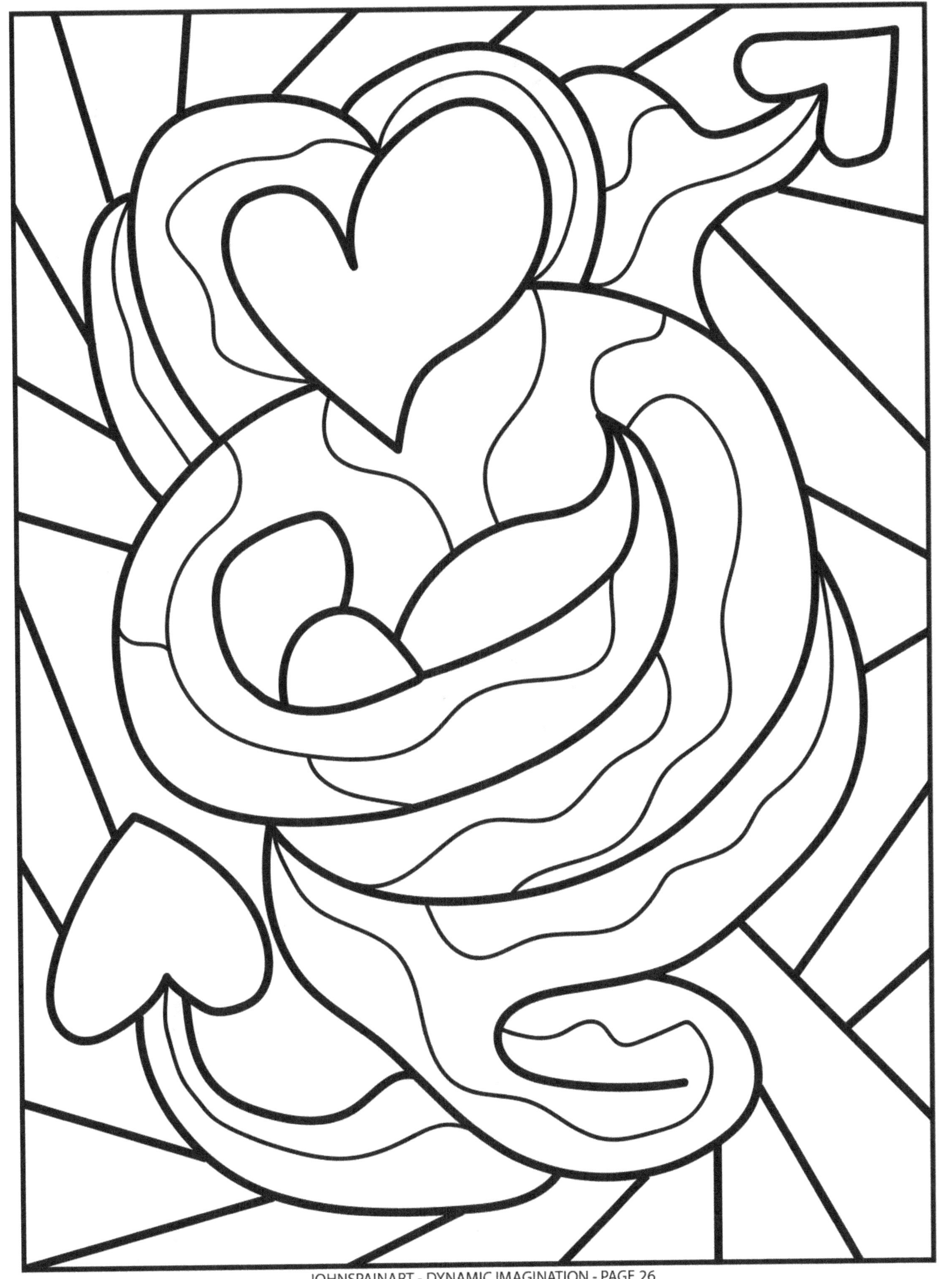

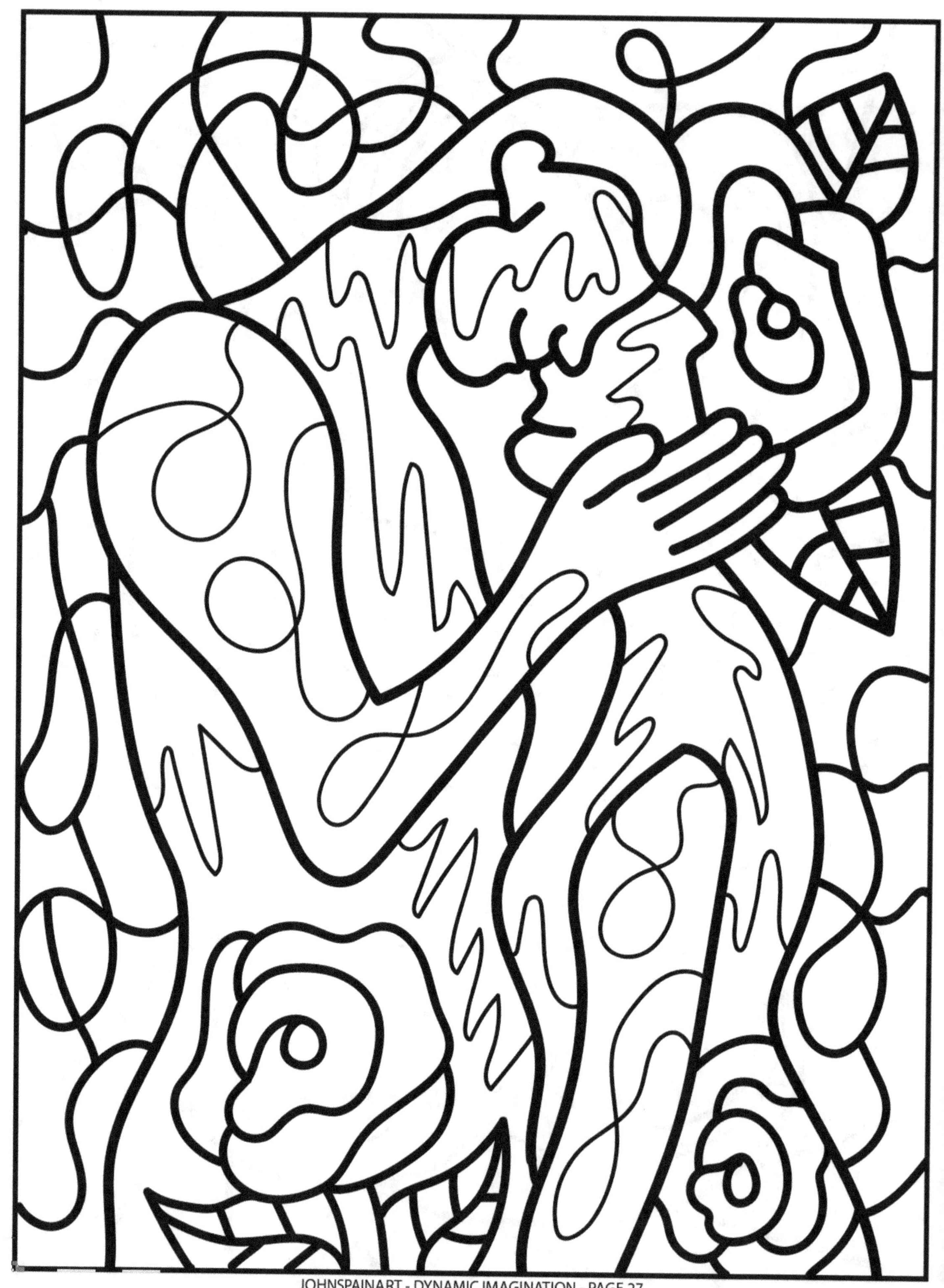

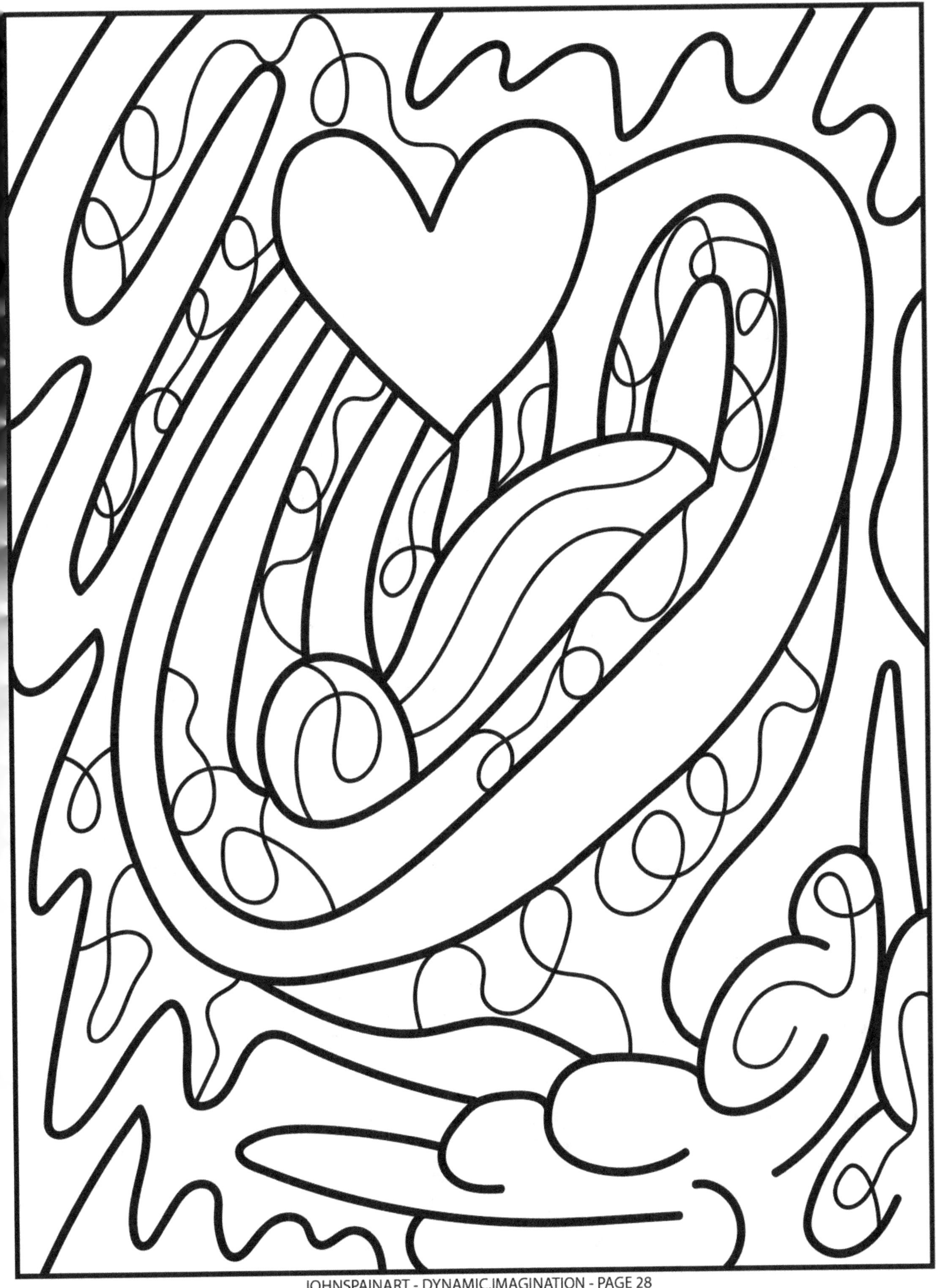

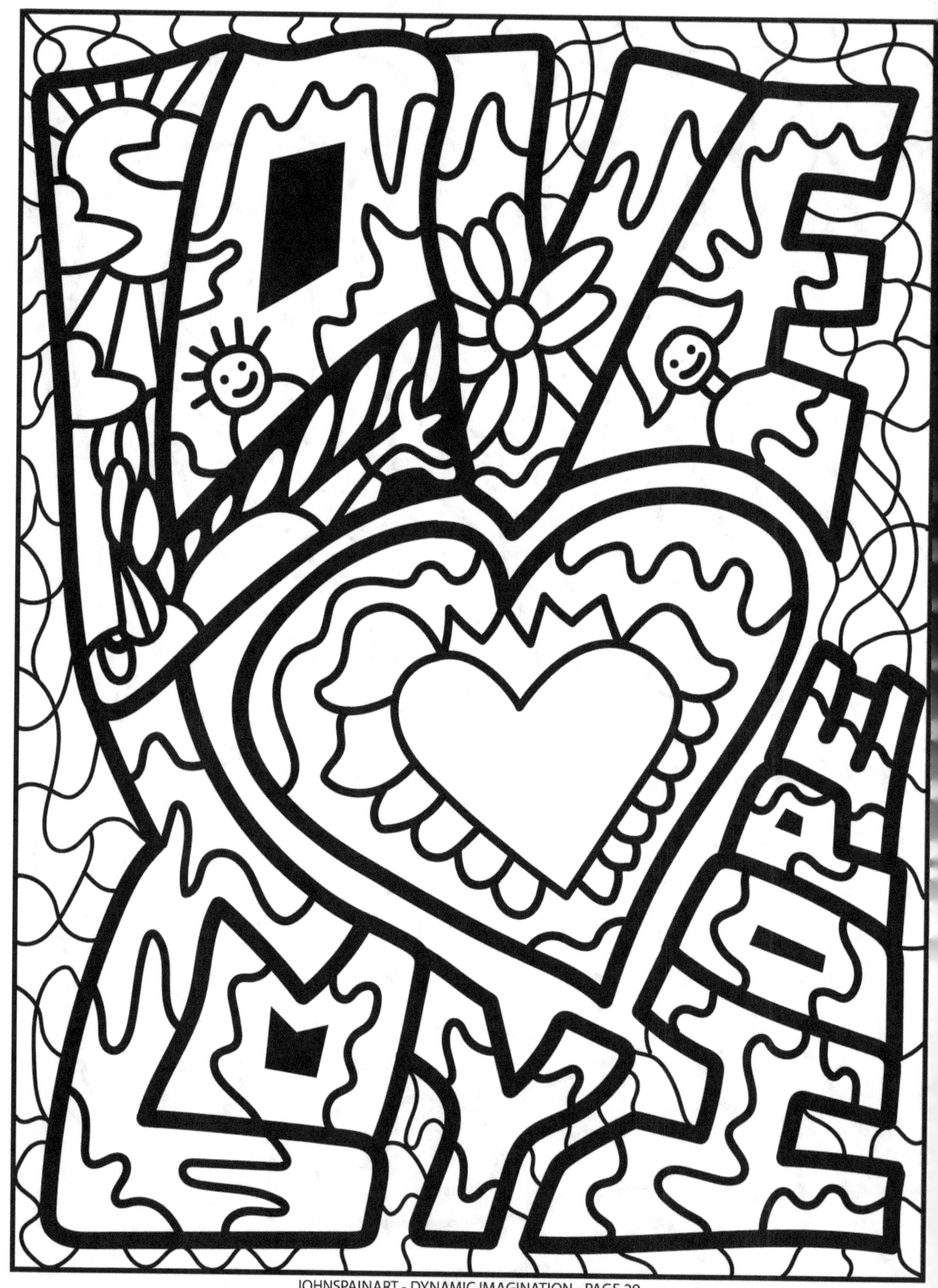

LOVE

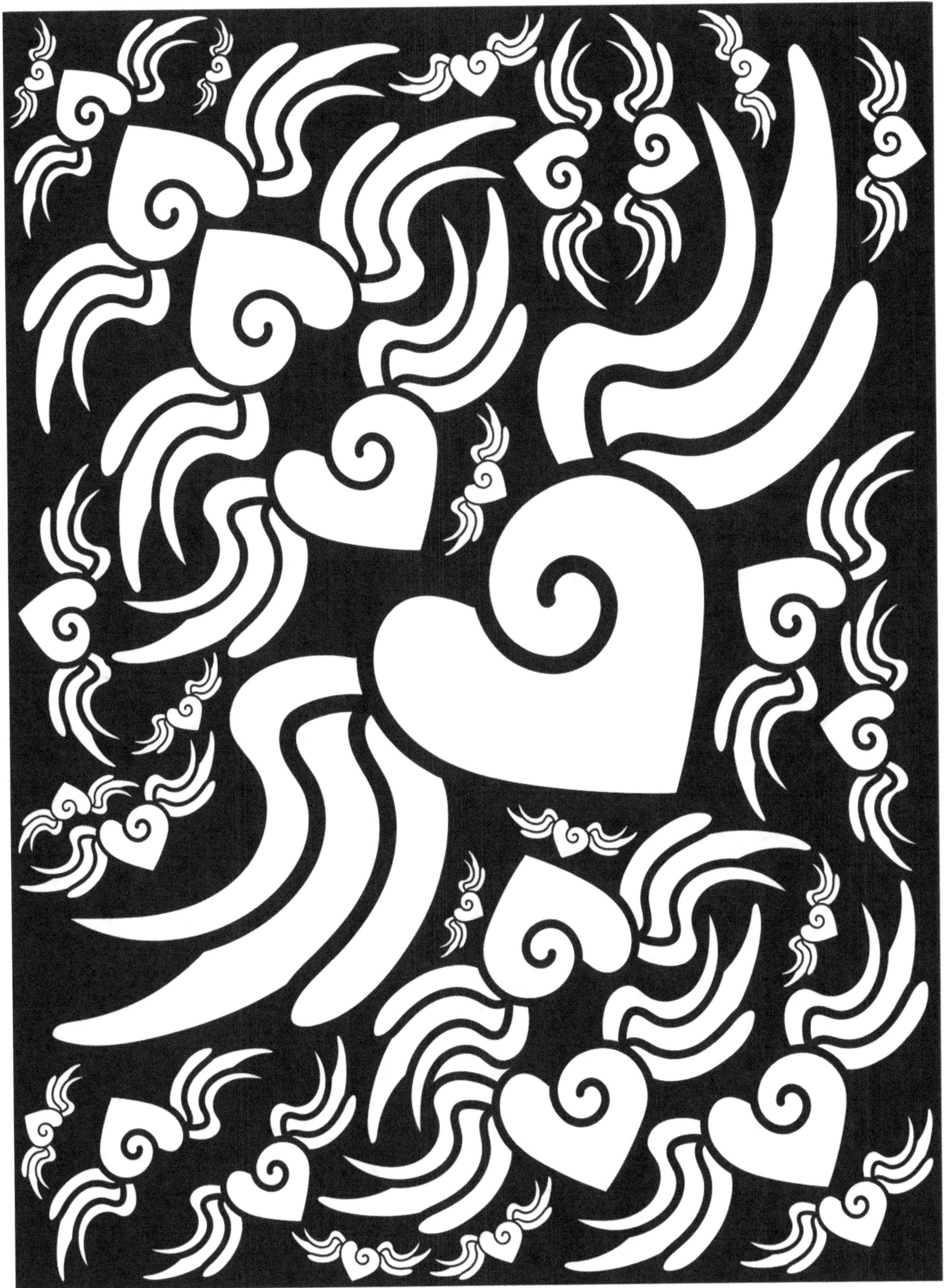

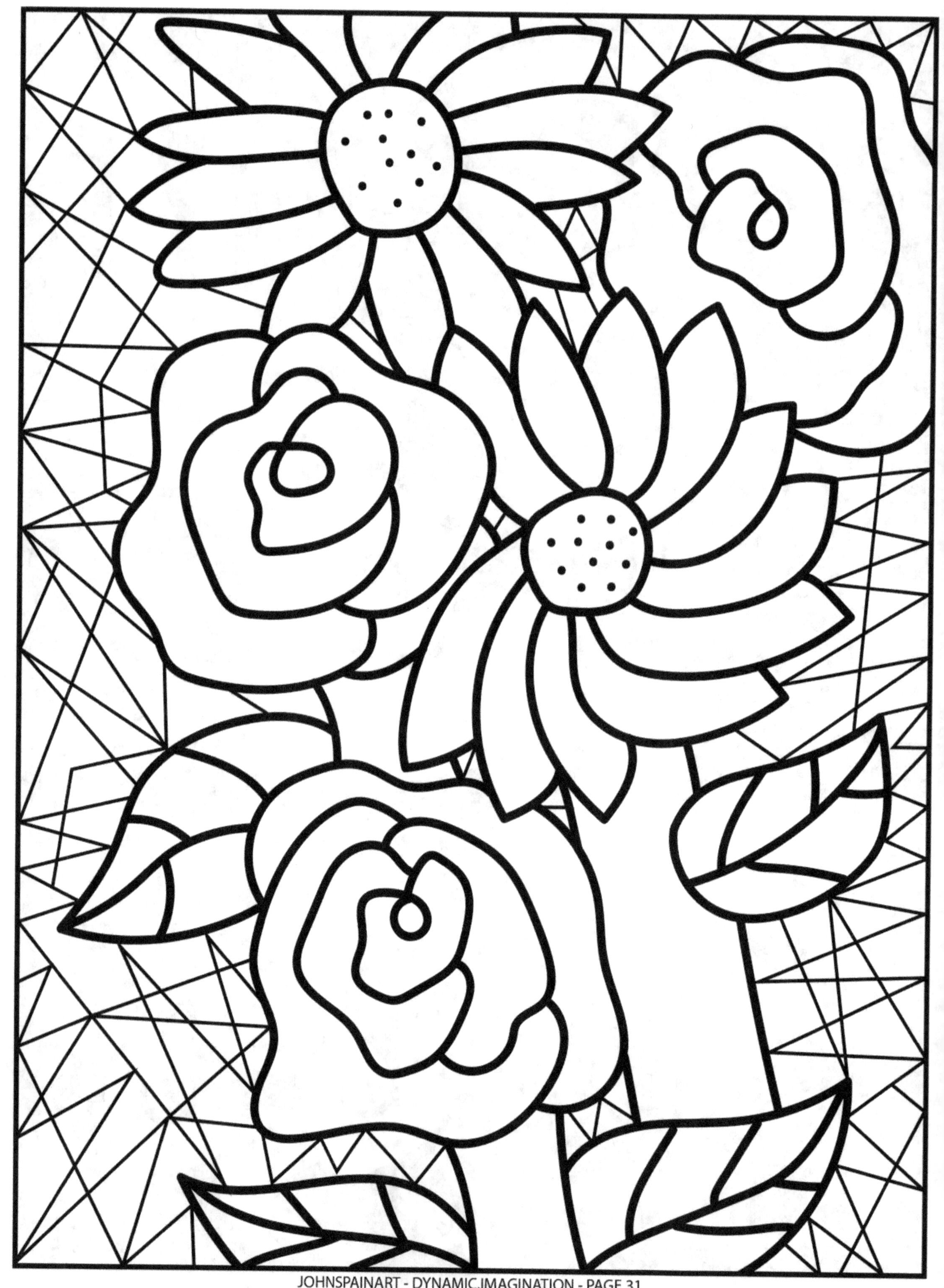

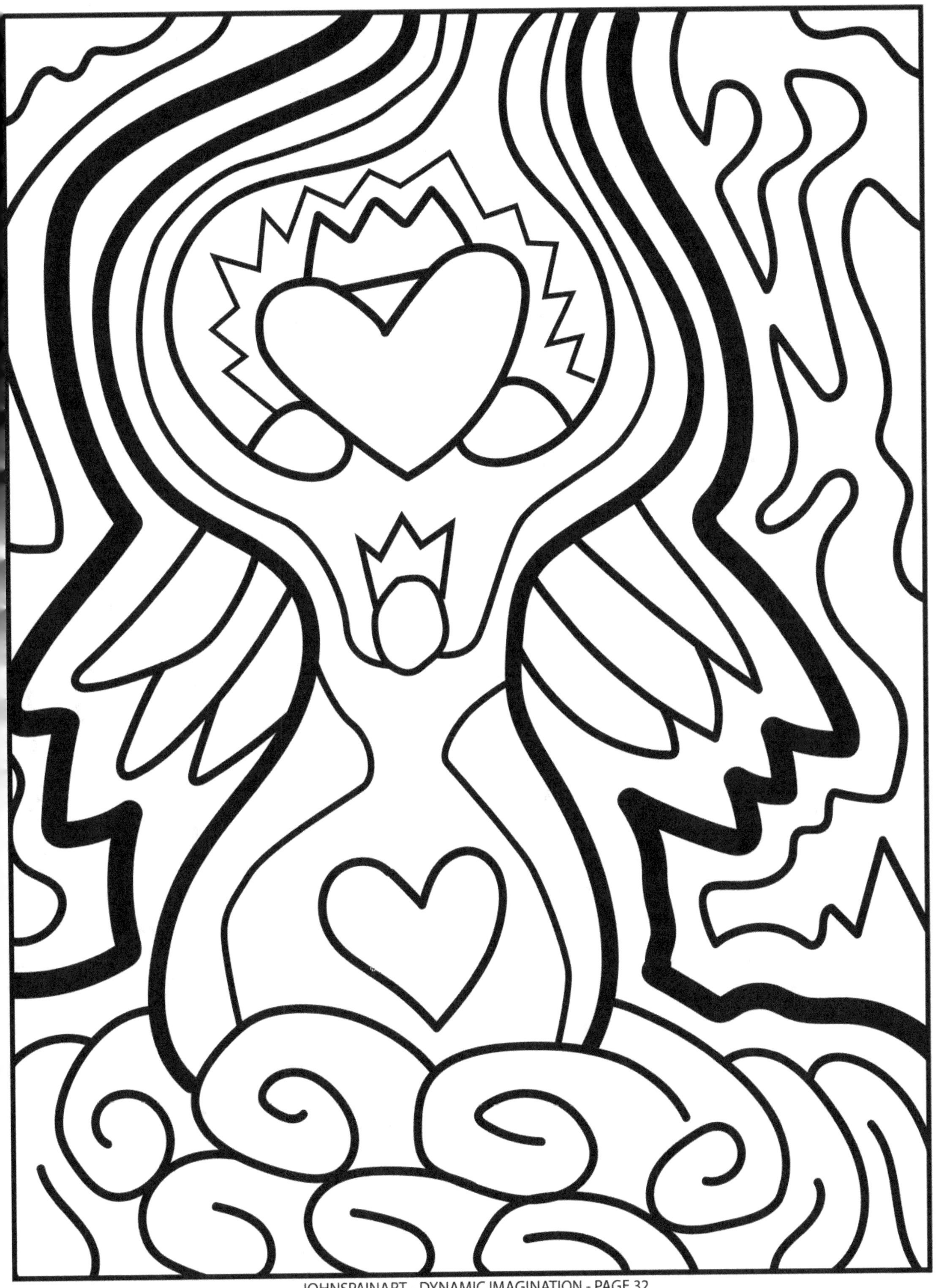

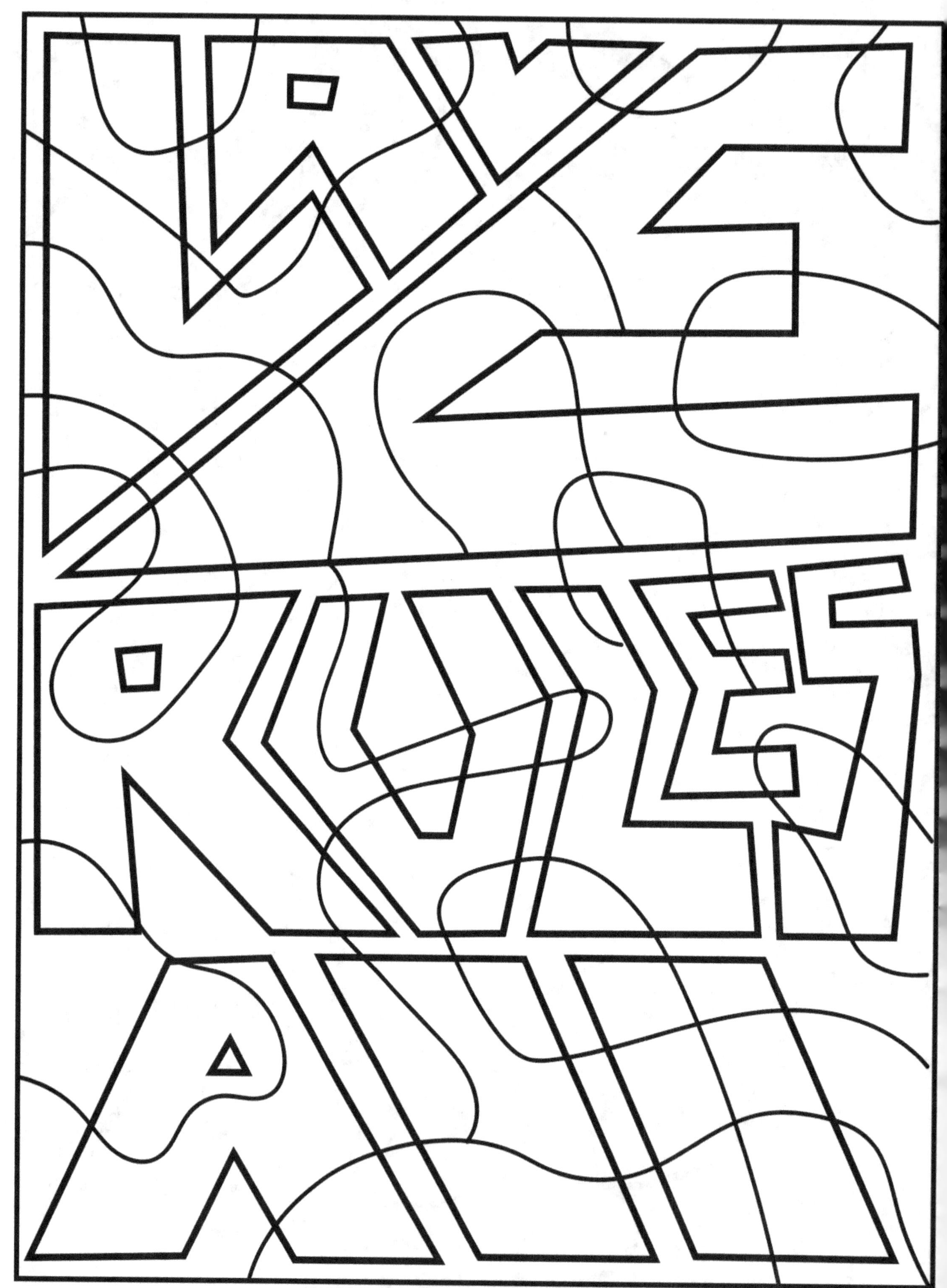

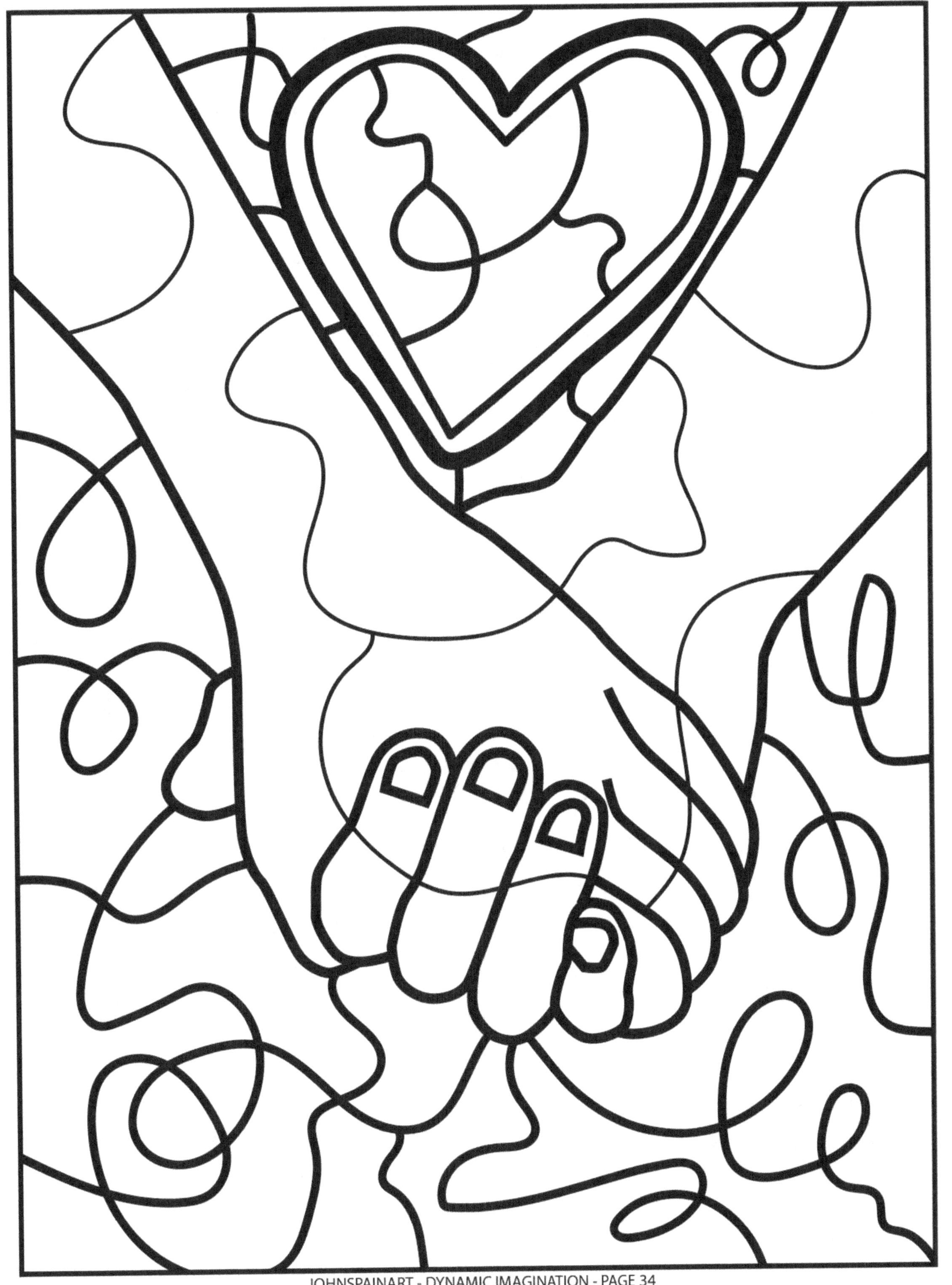

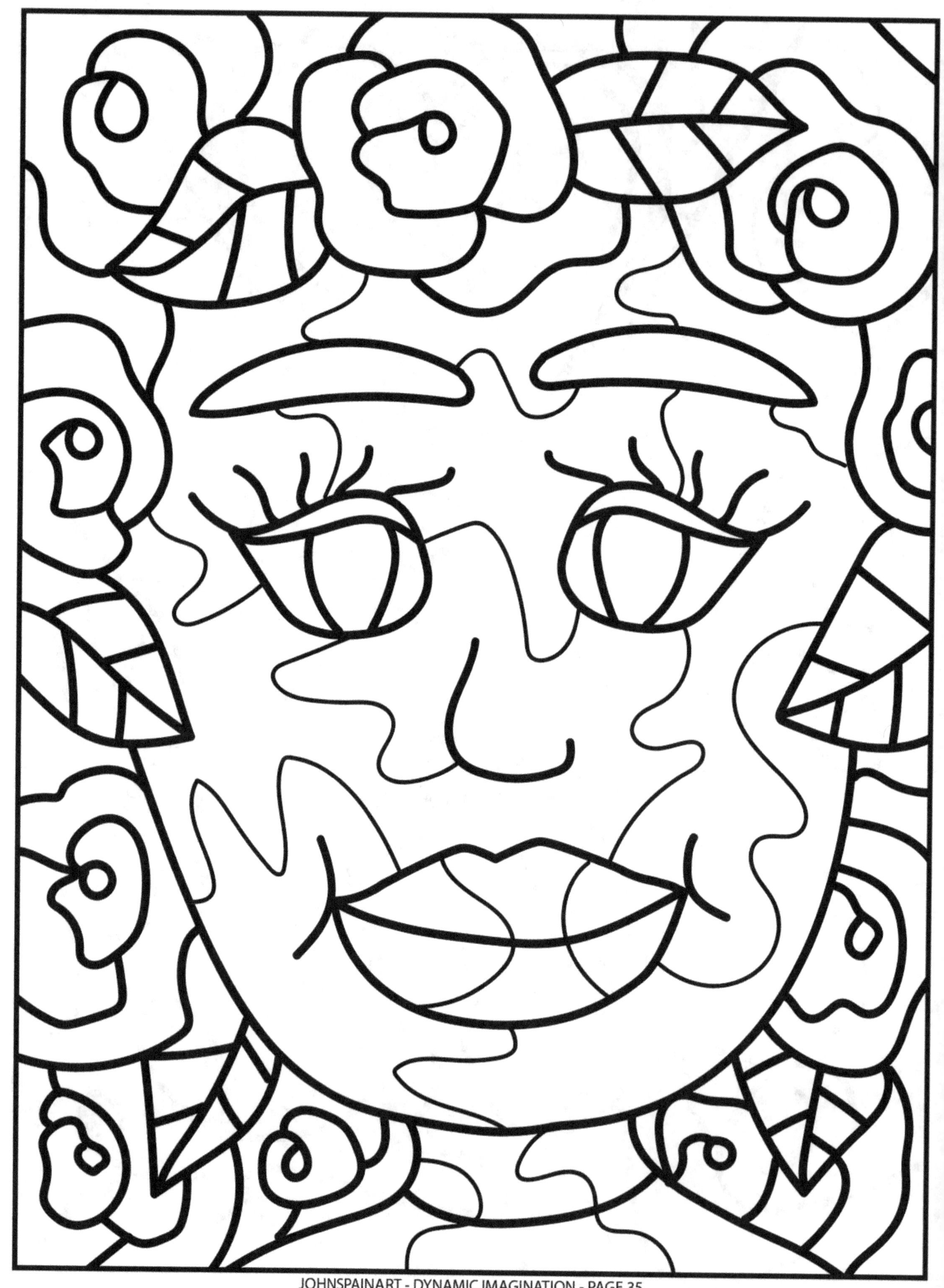

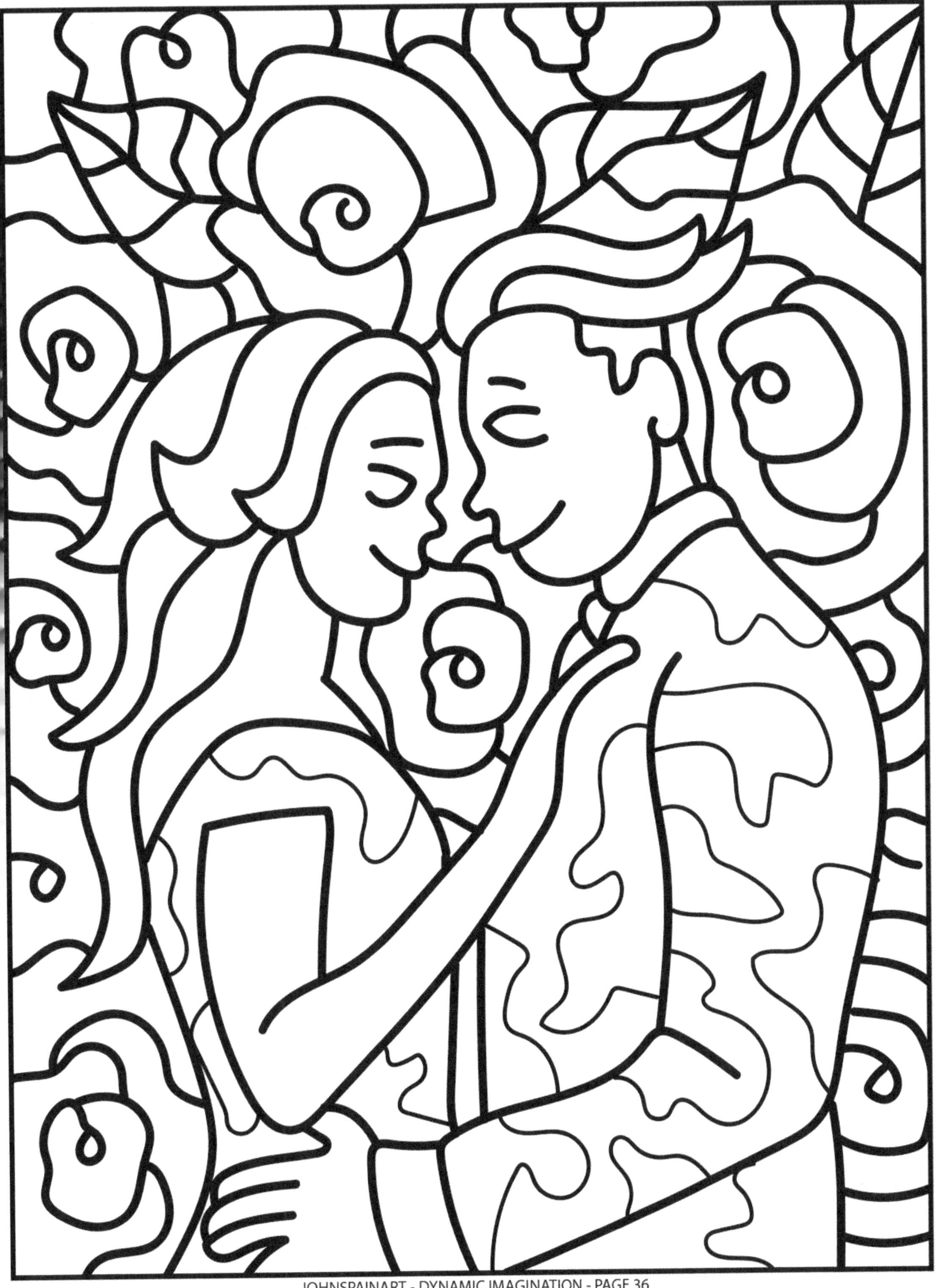

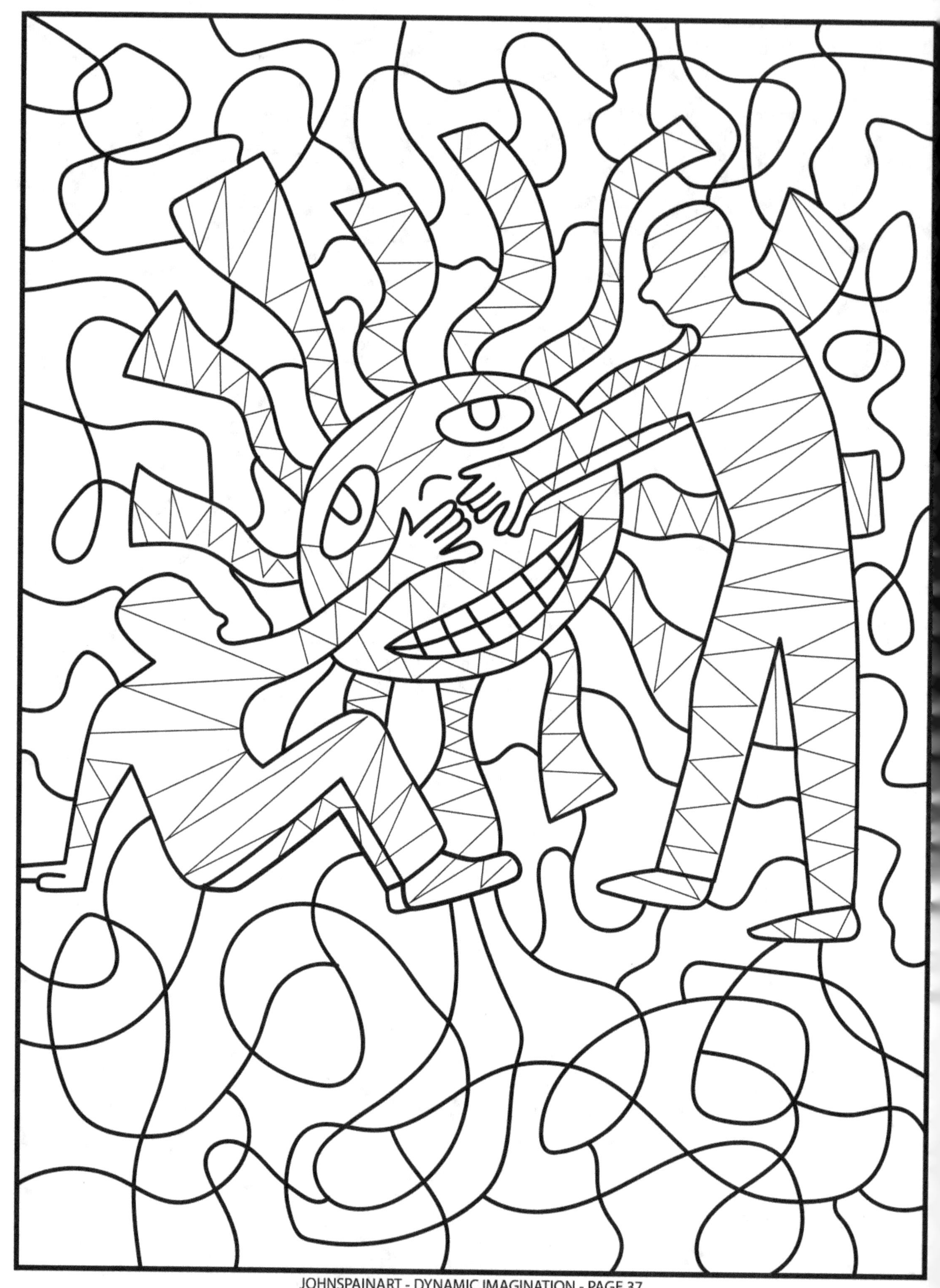

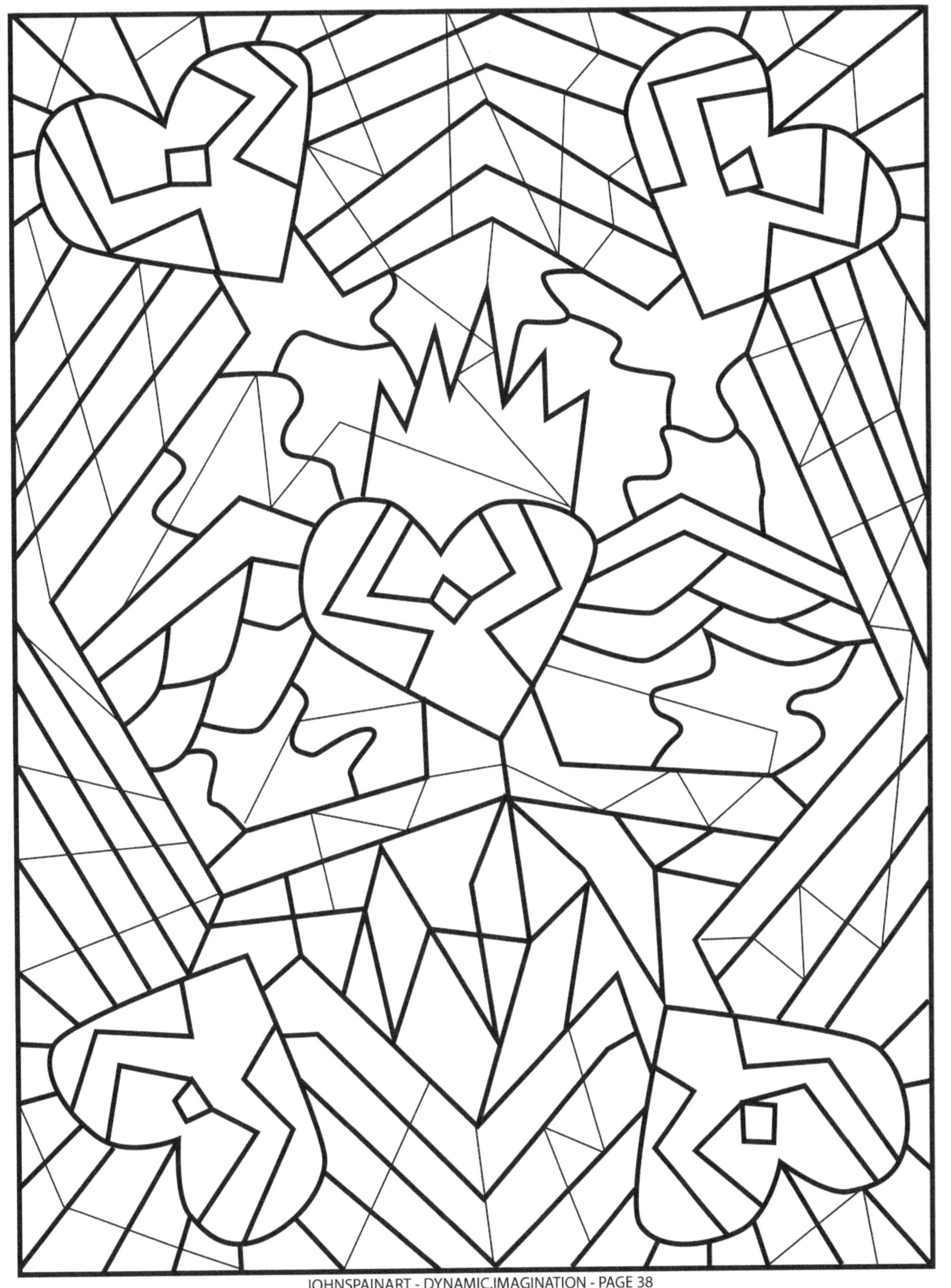

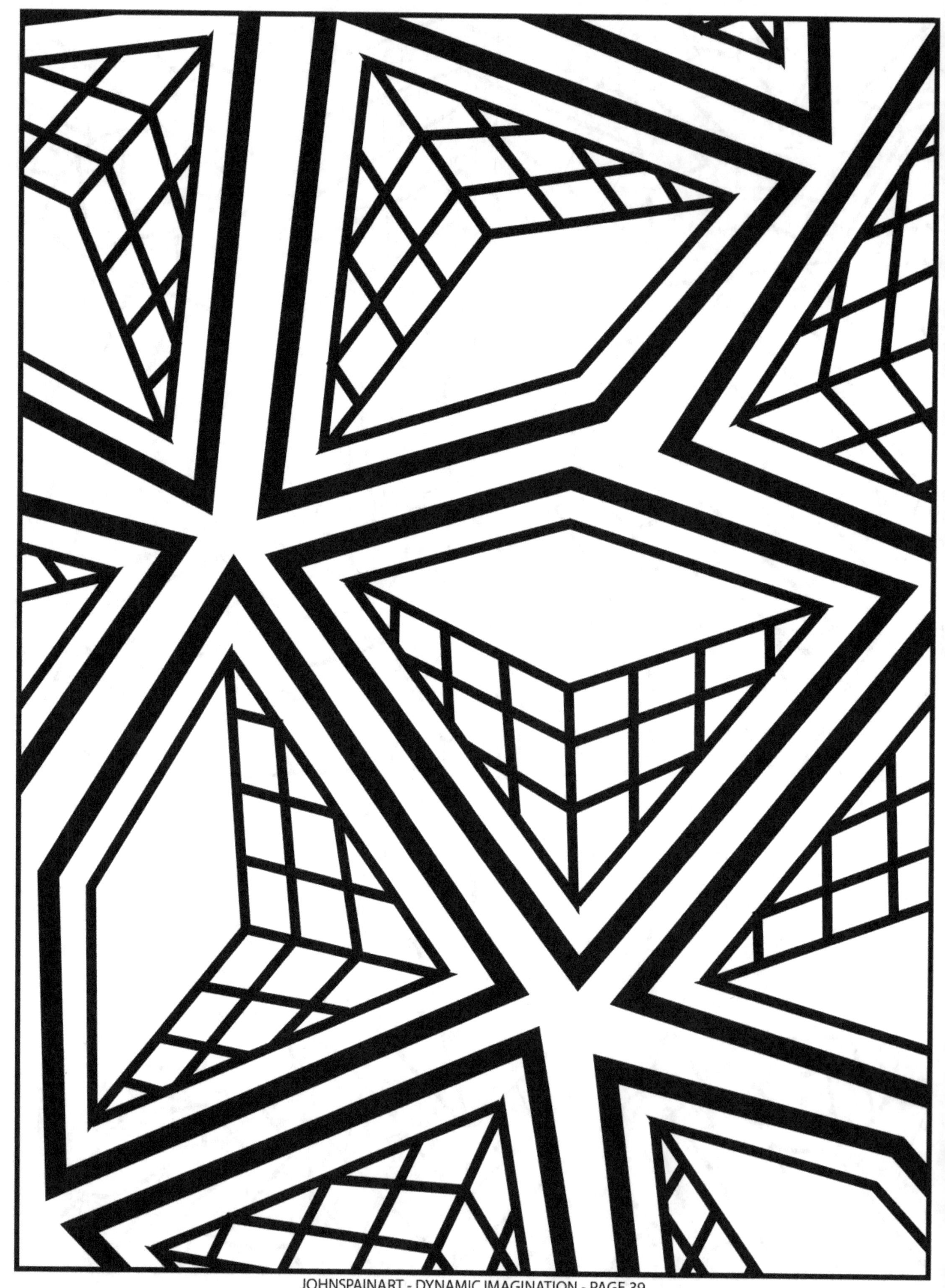

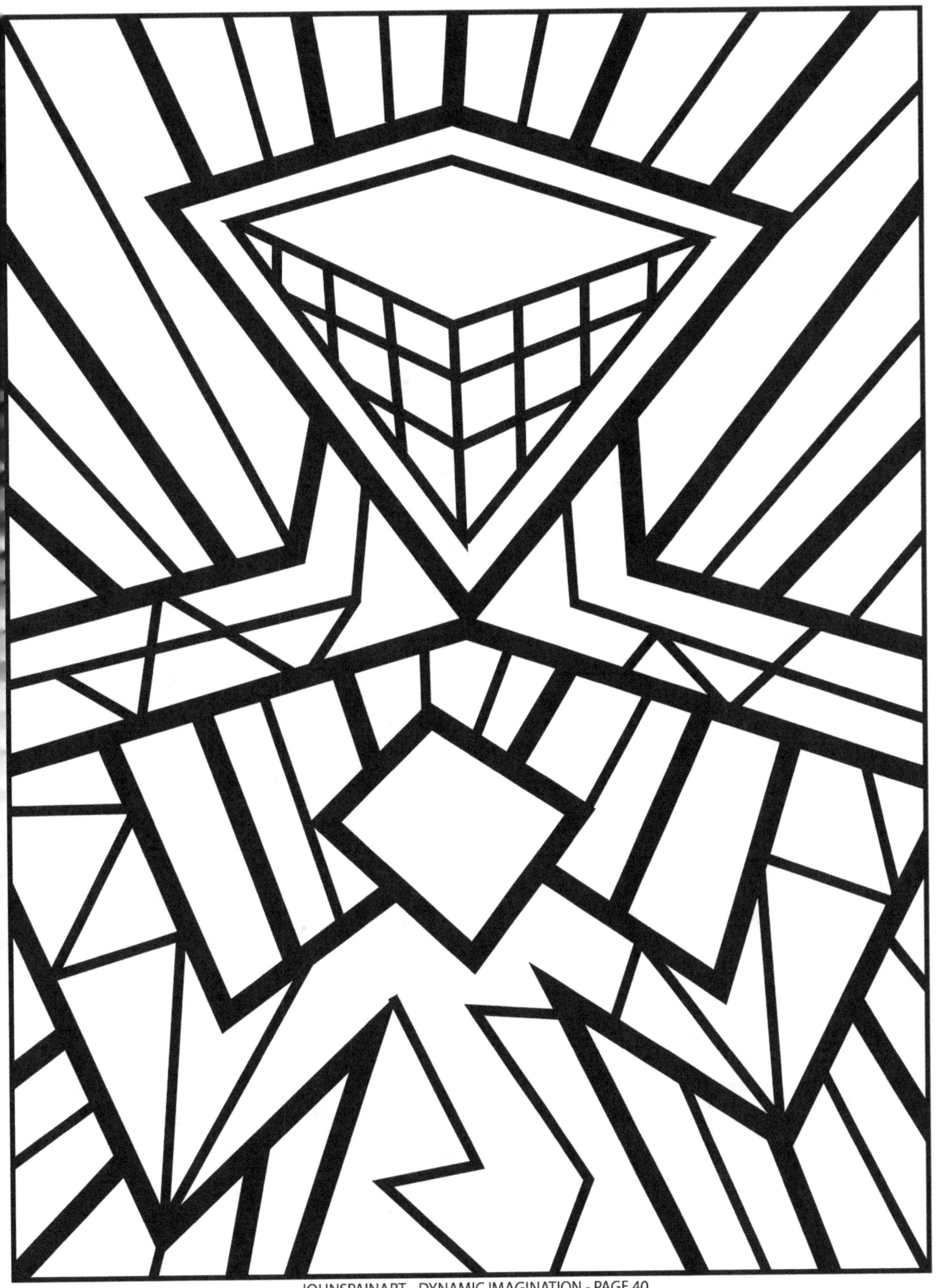

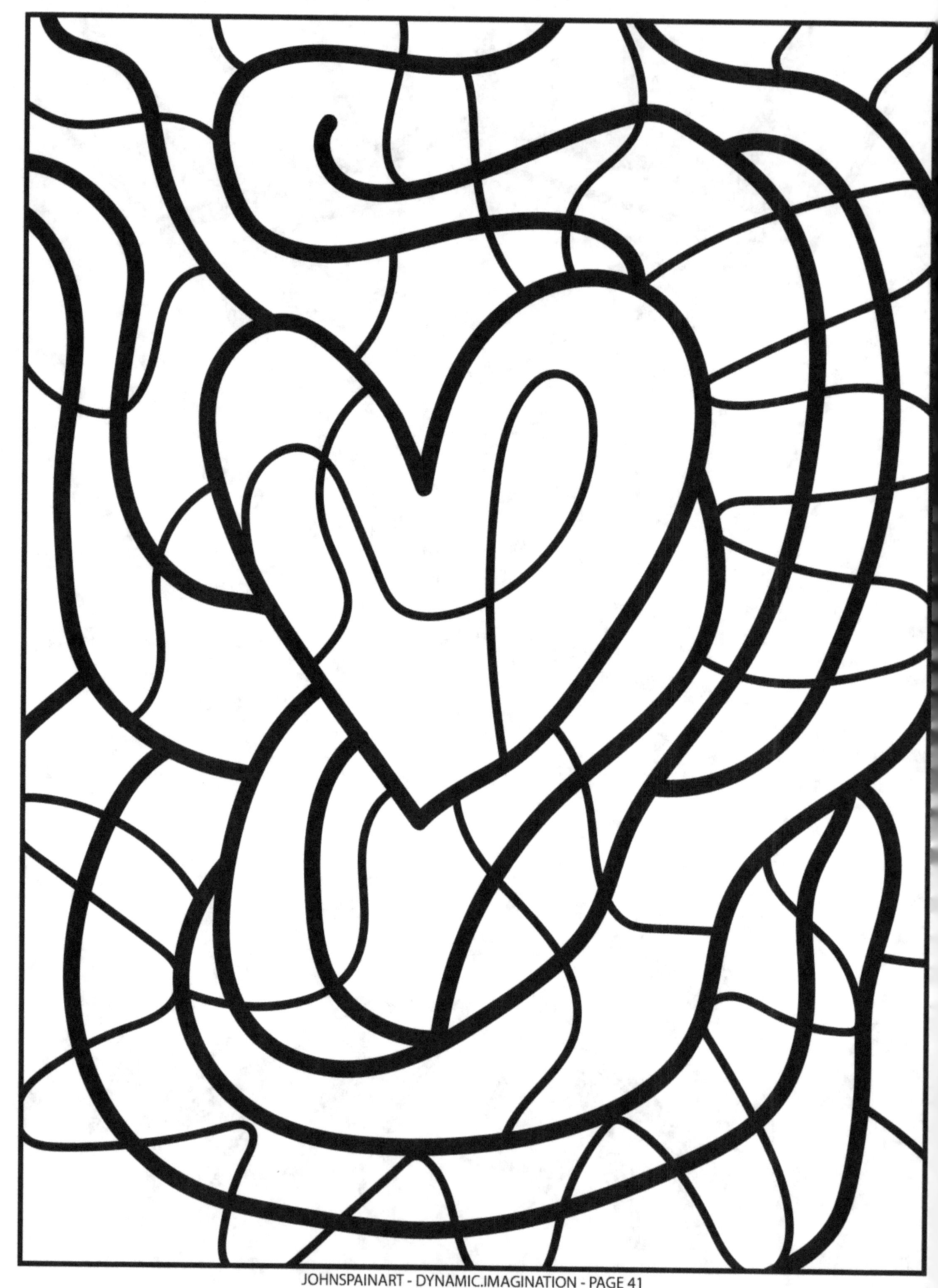

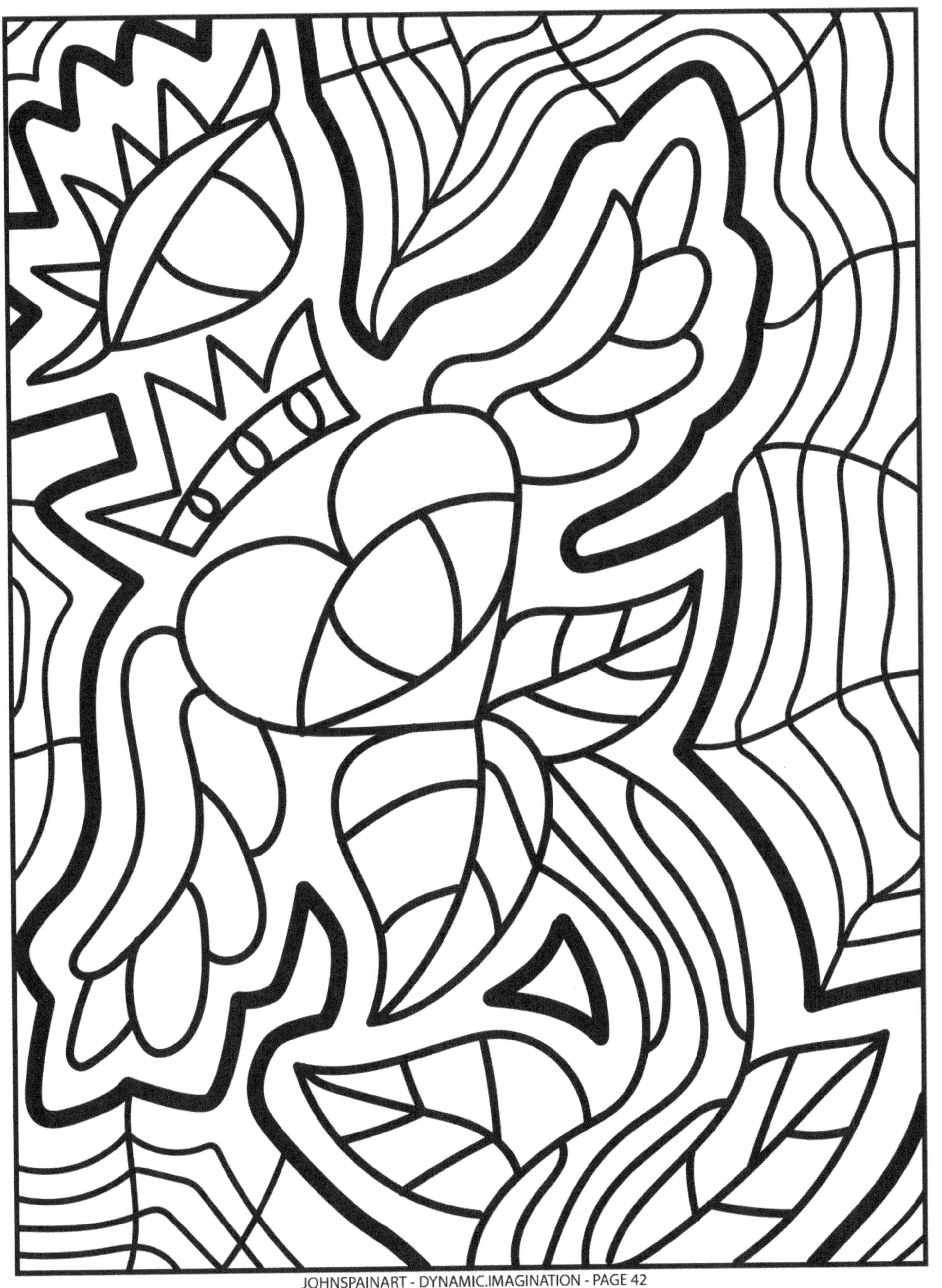

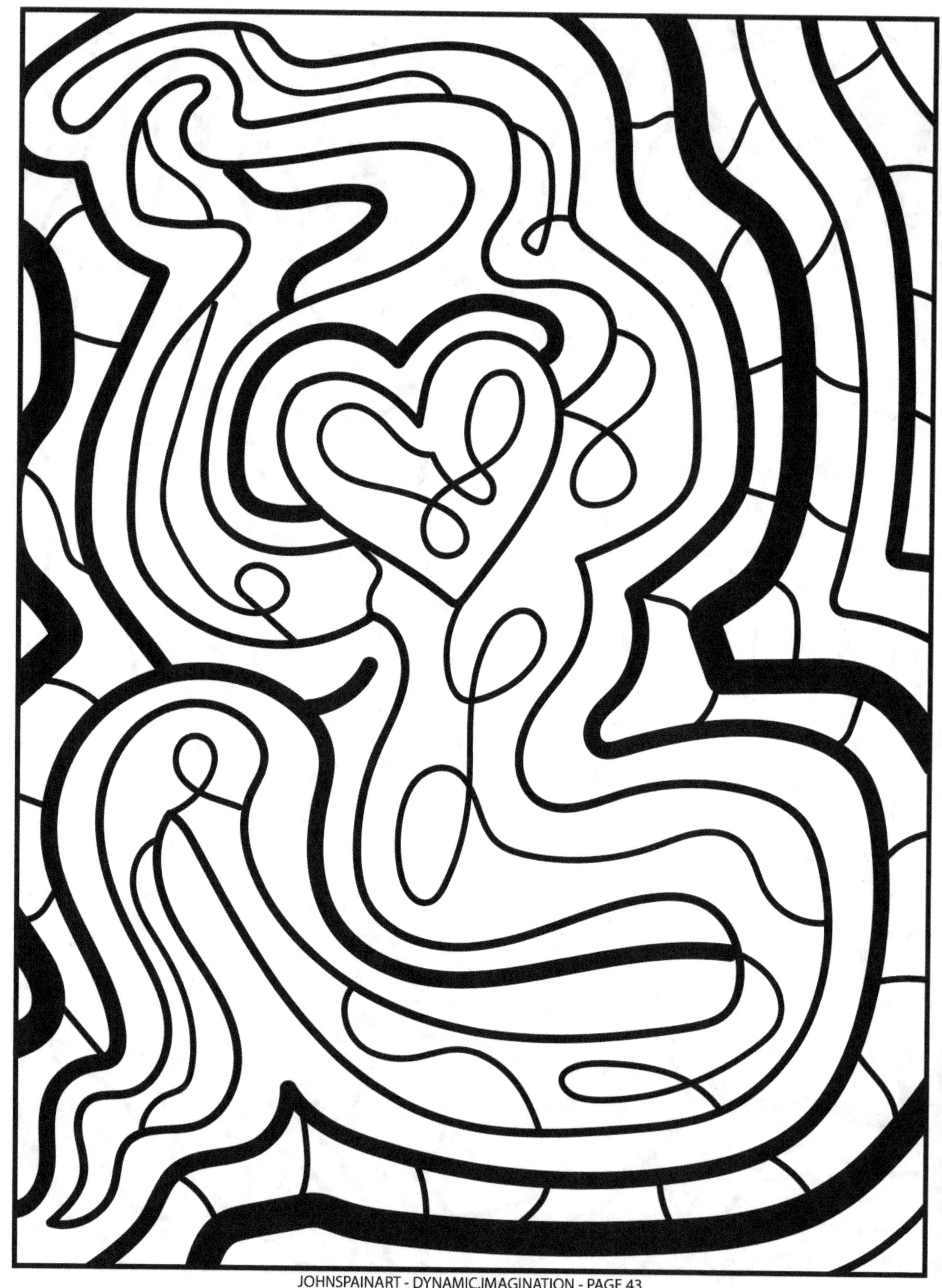

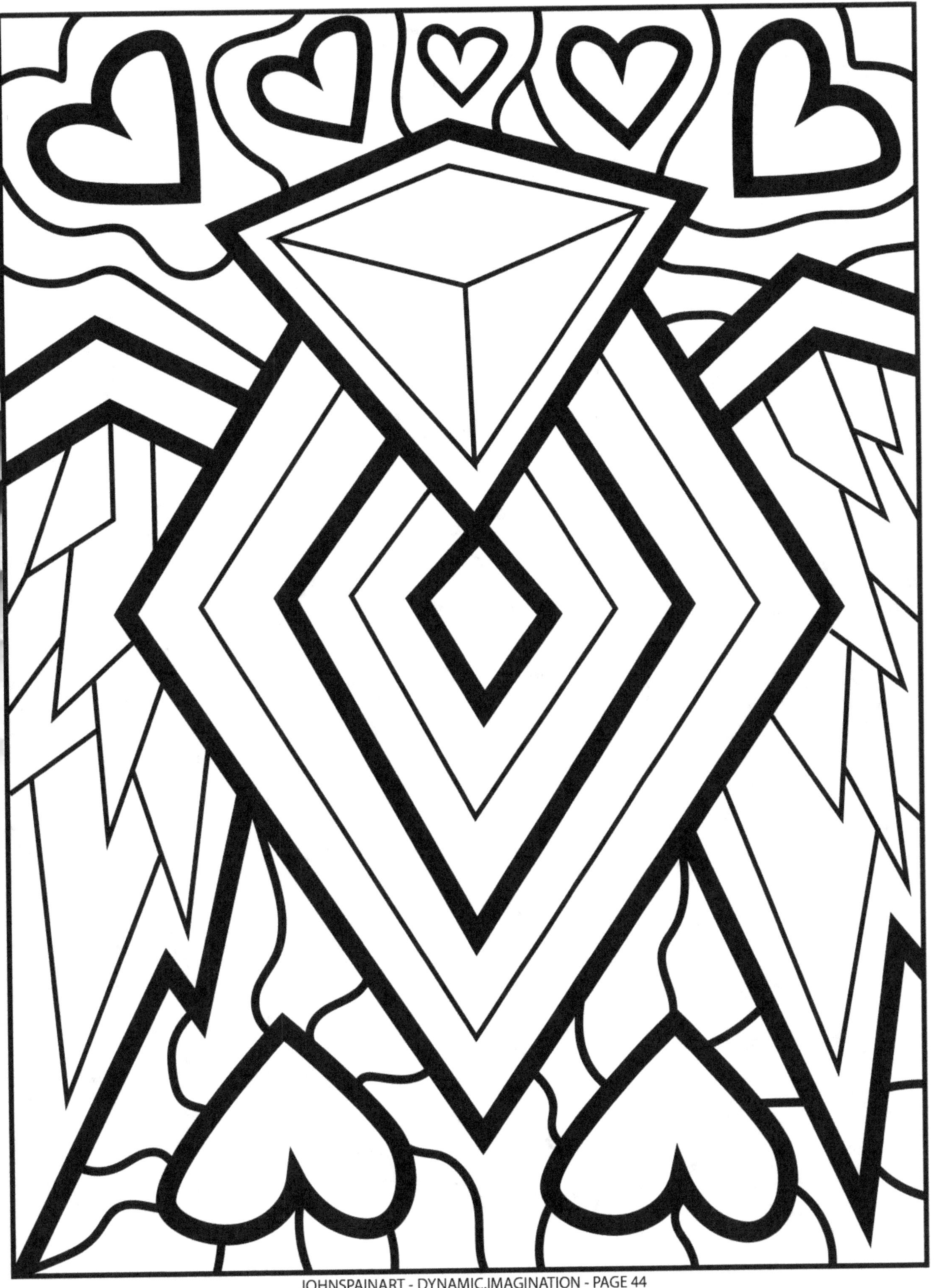

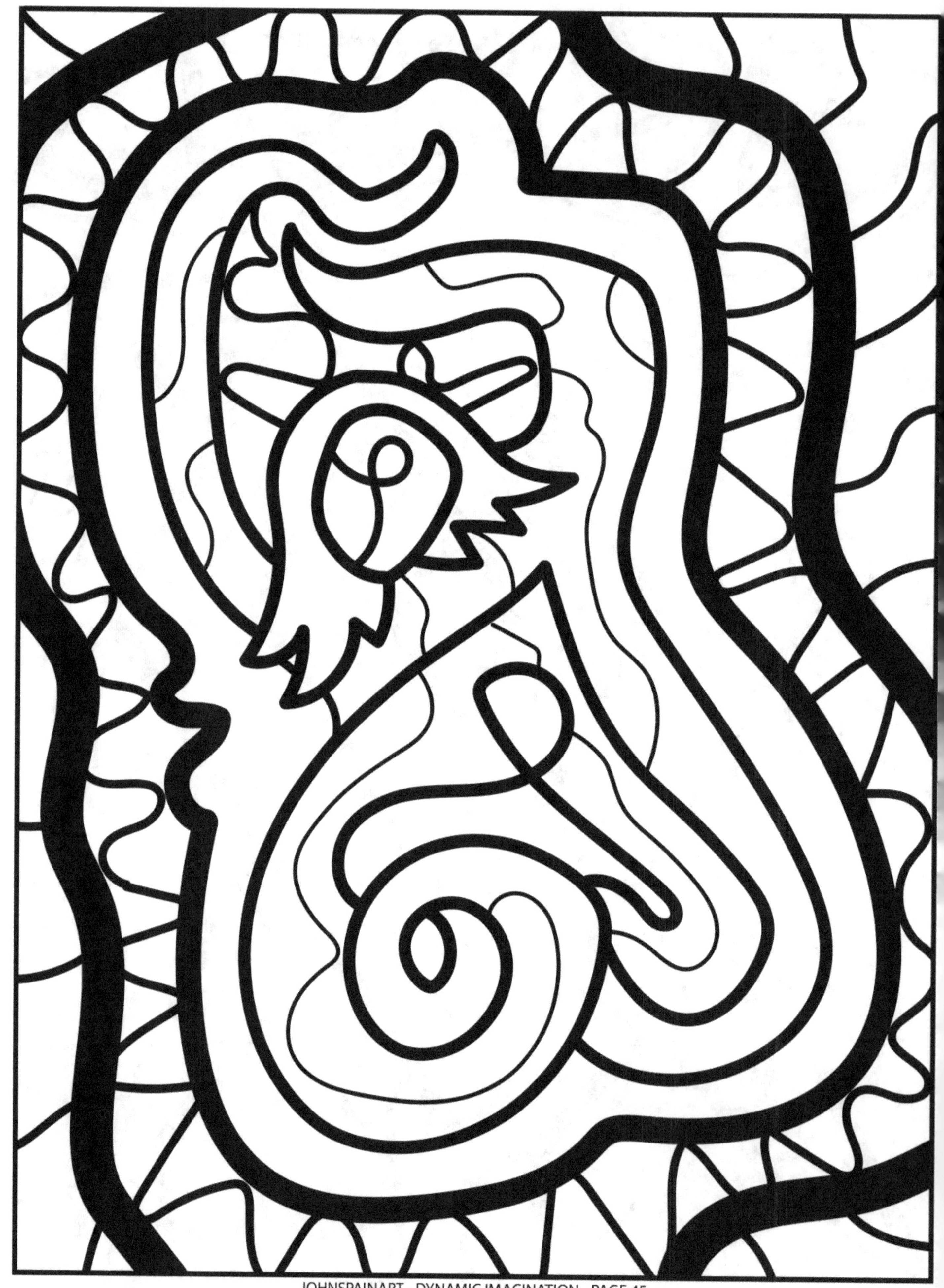

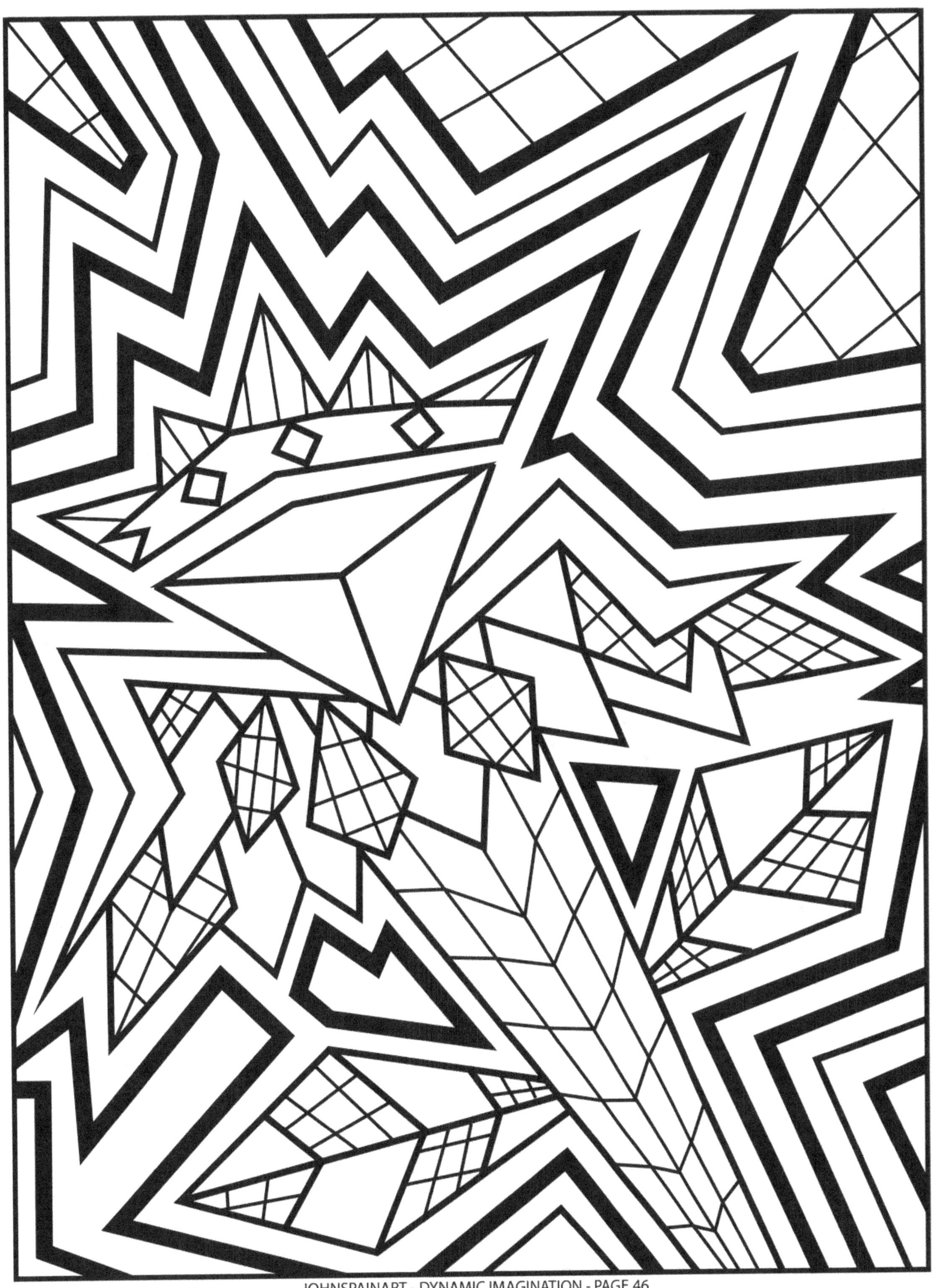

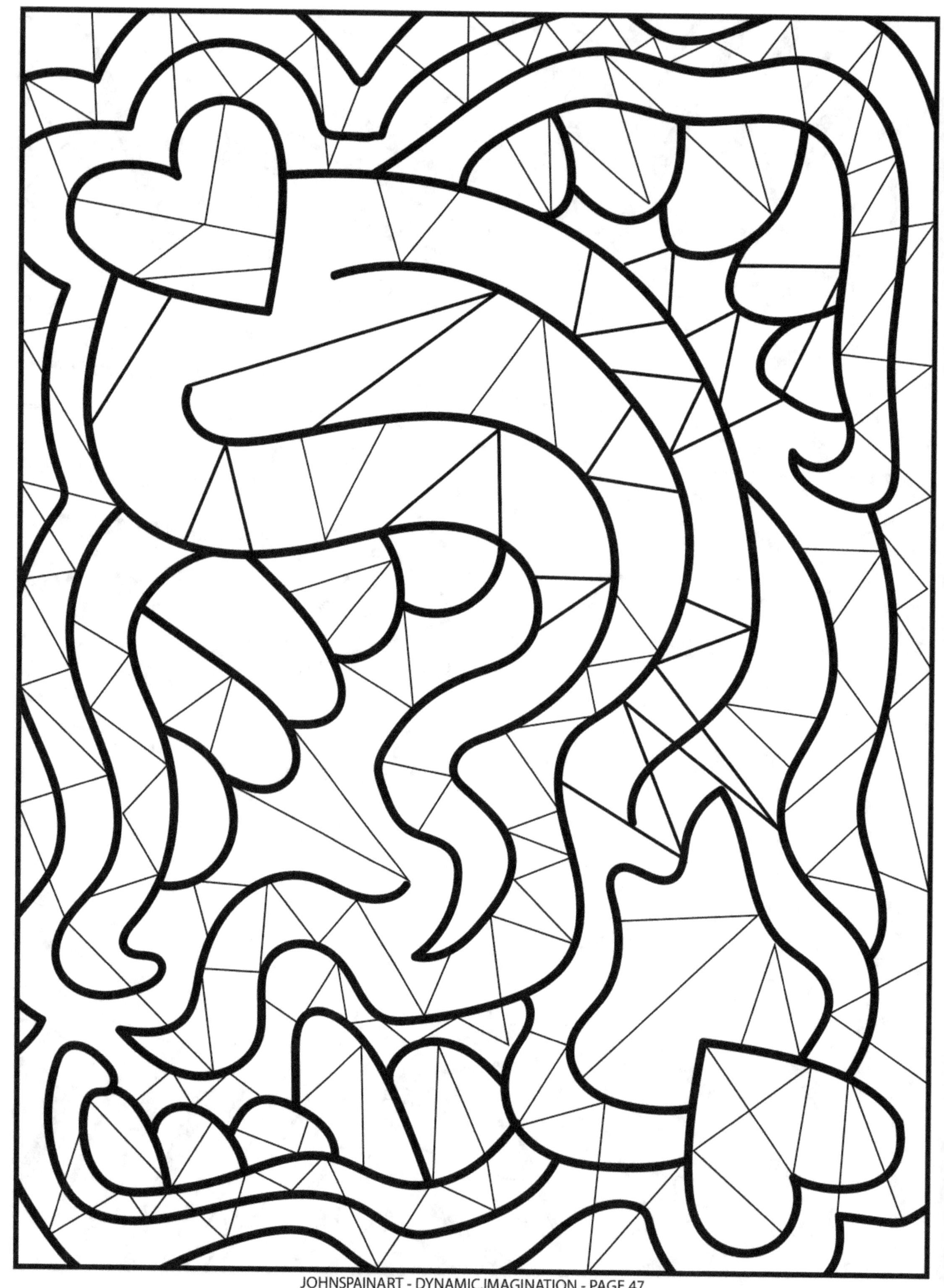

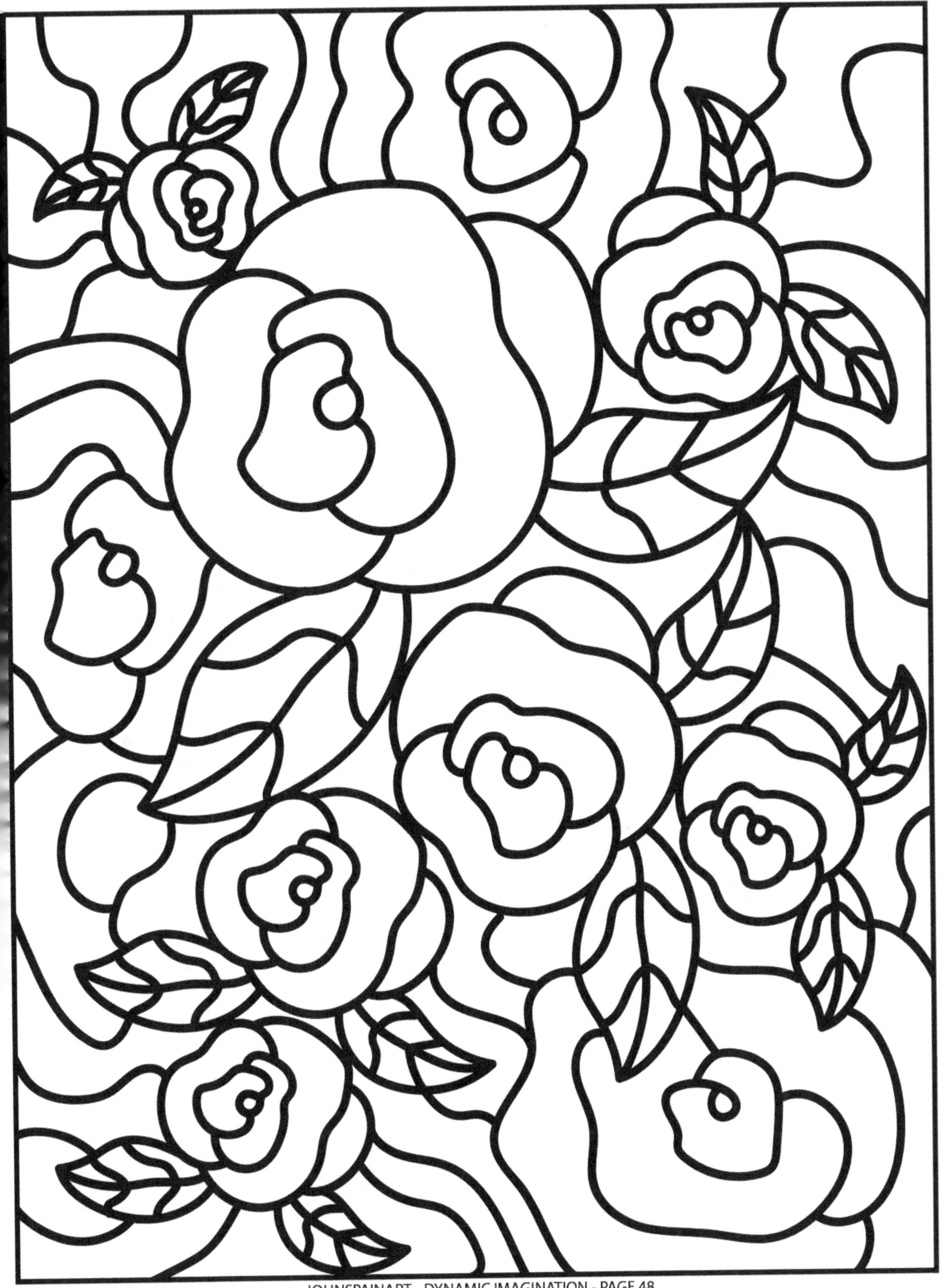

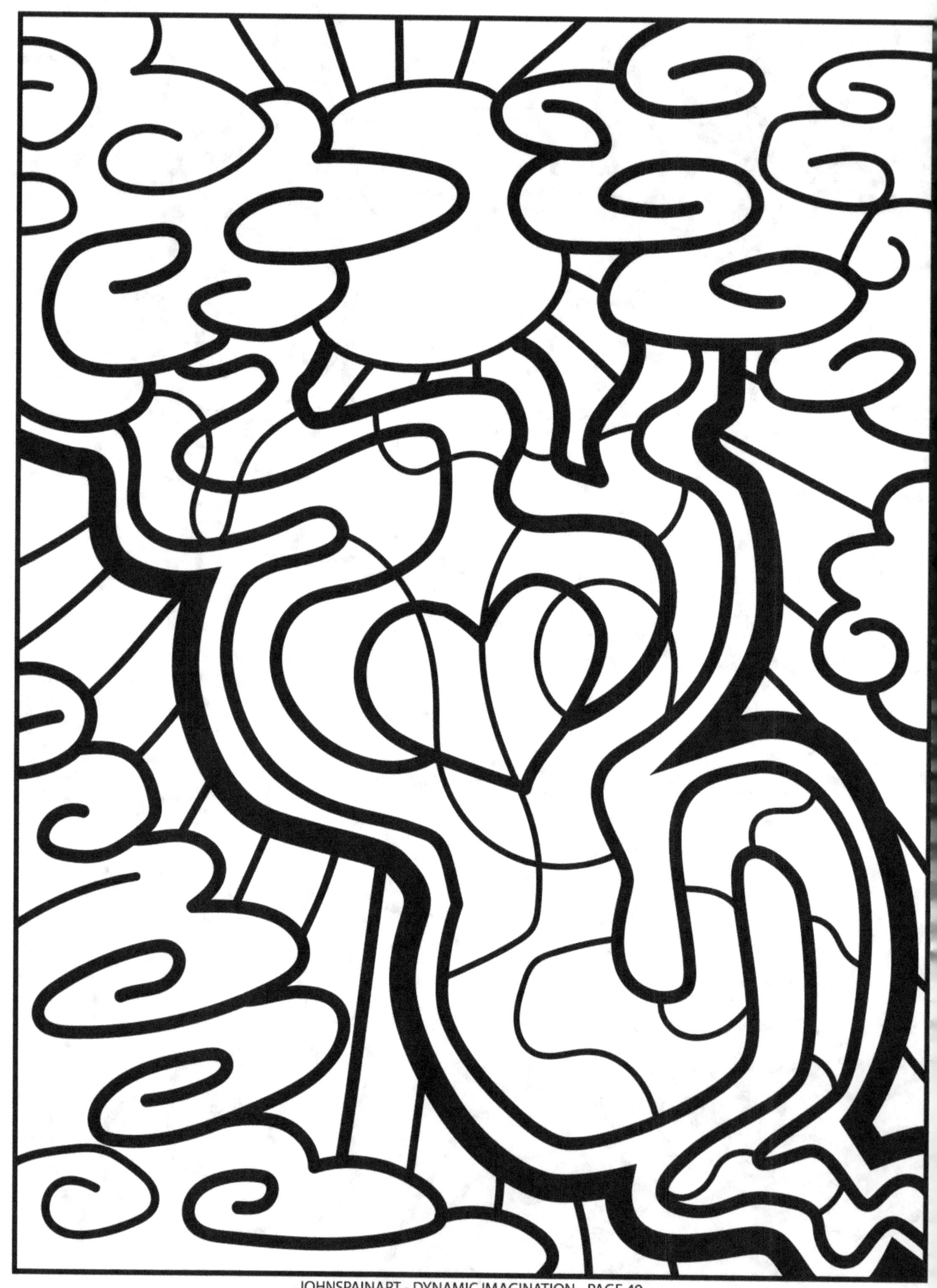

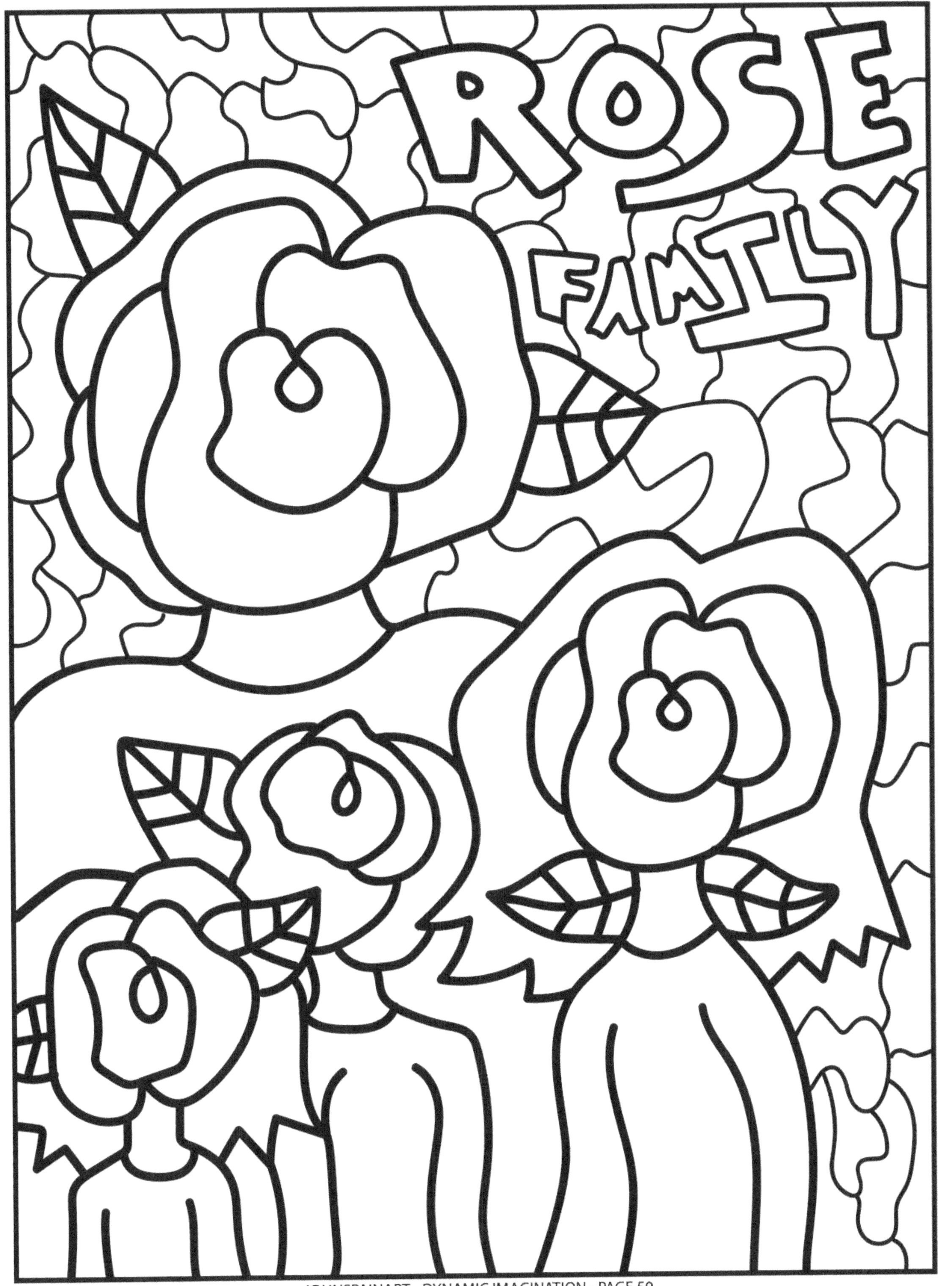

ROSE
FAMILY

www.ingramcontent.com/pod-product-compliance
Lightning Source LLC
Chambersburg PA
CBHW080922260726
48661CB00009B/3773